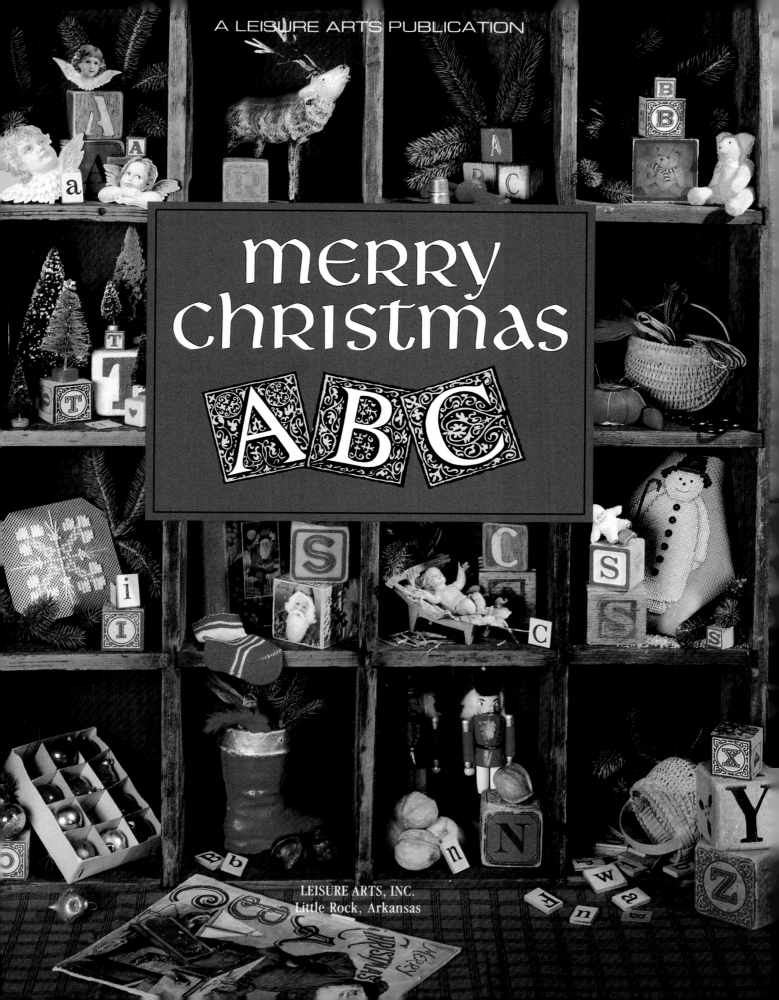

A LEISURE ARTS PUBLICATION

MERRY CHRISTMAS
ABC

LEISURE ARTS, INC.
Little Rock, Arkansas

EDITORIAL STAFF

Editor-in Chief: Anne Van Wagner Childs. *Executive Director:* Sandra Graham Case. *Executive Editor:* Susan Frantz Wiles. *Publications Director:* Carla Bentley. *Creative Art Director:* Gloria Bearden. *Production Art Director:* Melinda Stout. PRODUCTION — *Managing Editor:* Susan White Sullivan. *Senior Project Coordinator:* Kelley Pillow Taylor. *Project Coordinator:* Carla A. Jones. DESIGN — *Design Director:* Patricia Wallenfang Sowers. *Designer:* Linda Diehl Tiano. EDITORIAL — *Associate Editor:* Dorothy Latimer Johnson. *Senior Editor:* Linda L. Trimble. *Editorial Writer:* Laurie S. Rodwell. *Advertising and Direct Mail Copywriters:* Steven M. Cooper, Marla Shivers, and Tena Kelley Vaughn. ART — *Book/Magazine Art Director:* Diane M. Ghegan. *Senior Production Artist:* Stephen L. Mooningham. *Chart Production Artists:* Martha Jordan, Ashley S. Cole, Guniz Ustun, Hubrith Esters, and M. Katherine Yancey. *Creative Art Assistant:* Judith Howington Merritt. *Photography Stylists:* Charlisa Erwin Parker and Christina Tiano. *Typesetters:* Cindy Lumpkin and Stephanie Cordero. *Advertising and Direct Mail Artists:* Linda Lovette and Jeff Curtis.

BUSINESS STAFF

Publisher: Steve Patterson. *Controller:* Tom Siebenmorgen. *Retail Sales Director:* Richard Tignor. *Retail Marketing Director:* Pam Stebbins. *Retail Customer Services Director:* Margaret Sweetin. *Marketing Manager:* Russ Barnett. *Executive Director of Marketing and Circulation:* Guy A. Crossley. *Fulfillment Manager:* Byron L. Taylor. *Print Production:* Nancy Reddick Lister and Laura Lockhart.

CREDITS

PHOTOGRAPHY: Ken West, Larry Pennington, and Karen Busick Shirey of Peerless Photography, Little Rock, Arkansas; and Jerry R. Davis of Jerry Davis Photography, Little Rock, Arkansas. COLOR SEPARATIONS: Magna IV Color Imaging of Little Rock, Arkansas. CUSTOM FRAMING: Nelda and Carlton Newby of Creative Framers, North Little Rock, Arkansas.

Library of Congress Catalog Number 93-78286
International Standard Book Number 0-942237-27-7

INTRODUCTION

When we discovered a turn-of-the-century children's book tucked away in a dusty antique shop, we were unexpectedly whisked away to a world of old-fashioned Christmas pleasures. The tiny volume, titled "Merry Christmas ABC," featured an enchanting Victorian alphabet poem accompanied by beautifully detailed illustrations. Inspired by this charming memento of yesteryear, we created our own delightful book of cross stitch creations depicting the joys of Christmas from A to Z.

A is for Angel adorning the tree.
B is for Bells that chime out in glee.
C is for Candy to please girls and boys.
D is for Dreams which we truly enjoy.
E is for Evergreens decking the room.
F is for Flowers of sweetest perfume.
G is for Gifts that bring us delight.
H is for Holly with red berries bright.
I is for Ice, winter's delicate art.
J for the Joy that sings in our hearts.
K is Kriss Kringle with fur cap and coat.
L is for Letters the children all wrote.
M is for Mistletoe inviting a kiss.
N for the Night that brought us such bliss.
O is for Ornaments; ooh's and aah's they attract.
P is for Peddler just opening his pack.
Q the Quadrille in which each one must dance.
R for the Reindeer that gallop and prance.
S is for Snow drifting down from above.
T is for Teddy, so easy to love.
U is for Uproar that goes on all day.
V is for Voices that carol a lay.
W for Wreaths hung up on the wall.
X is for Xmas with pleasures for all.
Y is for Yule-log that burns clear and bright.
Z is for Zest shown from morning till night.

TABLE OF

CONTENTS

A
is for
Angel
adorning
the tree.

Chart on pages 50-51.

is for Bells
that chime
out in
glee.

Chart on pages 52-53

C is for
Candy to
please girls
and boys.

D is for
Dreams
which we
truly enjoy.

Chart on pages 54-55

E is for Evergreens decking the room.

F is for Flowers of sweetest perfume.

Charts on pages 56-57

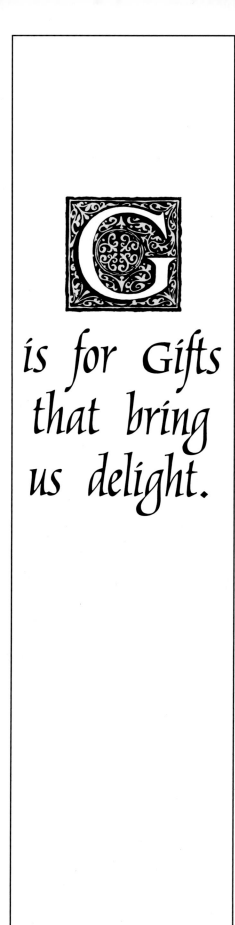

G is for Gifts
that bring
us delight.

14

A Christmas Recipe

Add to your meal some merriment
And a thought for Kith and Kin.
And then, as a prime ingredient,
A plenty of wit thrown in.
But spice it all with the essence
of love
And a little whiff of play.
Let a wise old book and a glance
above
Complete a well spent day.

Charts on pages 58-59

is for
Holly with
red berries
bright.

Chart on pages 60-61

I

is for Ice, winter's delicate art.

Charts on page 62

*for the
Joy that
sings in our
hearts.*

Chart on pages 64-65

 is Kriss Kringle with fur cap and coat.

 is for Letters the children all wrote.

Chart on pages 66-67

 is for
Mistletoe
inviting
a kiss.

Chart on page 63

for
the Night
that
brought us
such bliss.

*is for
Ornaments;
ooh's and
aah's they
attract.*

Charts on pages 70-71

P

*is for
Peddler just
opening his
pack.*

Chart on pages 72-73

Q

*the
Quadrille
in which
each one
must dance.*

Chart on pages 74-75

R for the Reindeer that gallop and prance.

Charts on pages 76-79

is for Snow drifting down from above.

Charts on pages 80-81

T is for Teddy, so easy to love.

Charts on pages 82-83

*is for
Uproar
that goes
on all day.*

Chart on pages 84-85

is for
Voices that
carol
a lay.

Charts on pages 86-87

W

for
Wreaths
hung up
on the
wall.

Charts on pages 88-89

*is for
Xmas with
pleasures
for all.*

Chart on pages 92-93

is for
Yule-log
that burns
clear and
bright.

is for Zest
shown from
morning
till night.

Chart on pages 90-91

a is for angel

Angel Treetop Ornament (shown on page 7):
The design was stitched over 2 fabric threads on a 10" x 14" piece of Cream Belfast Linen (32 ct) using 2 strands of floss for Cross Stitch, and 1 strand for Backstitch and French Knot.

For treetop ornament, cut one piece of Belfast Linen same size as stitched piece for backing. Matching arrows to form one pattern, trace entire treetop pattern (page 96) onto tracing paper; cut out pattern. Matching right sides and raw edges, pin stitched piece and backing fabric together. Center pattern on wrong side of stitched piece and use a fabric marking pencil to draw around pattern. Cut fabric pieces along drawn line; remove pins.

Cut one 28" length of purchased ¼" dia. cording. If needed, trim seam allowance of cording to ½". Matching raw edges and beginning and ending at bottom edge of stitched piece, baste cording to right side of stitched piece.

Matching right sides and raw edges and leaving bottom edge open, use a zipper foot and ½" seam allowance to sew stitched piece and backing fabric together. Clip curves and turn right side out, carefully pushing curves outward. Press bottom edge ½" to wrong side. Stuff with polyester fiberfill and whipstitch bottom edge closed.

For ties, cut two 18" lengths of ¼"w ribbon. Fold each length in half and whipstitch center of each length to back of treetop ornament 4" apart (**Fig. 1**).

Fig. 1

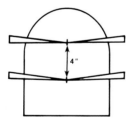

Needlework adaptation by Nancy Dockter and Carol Emmer.

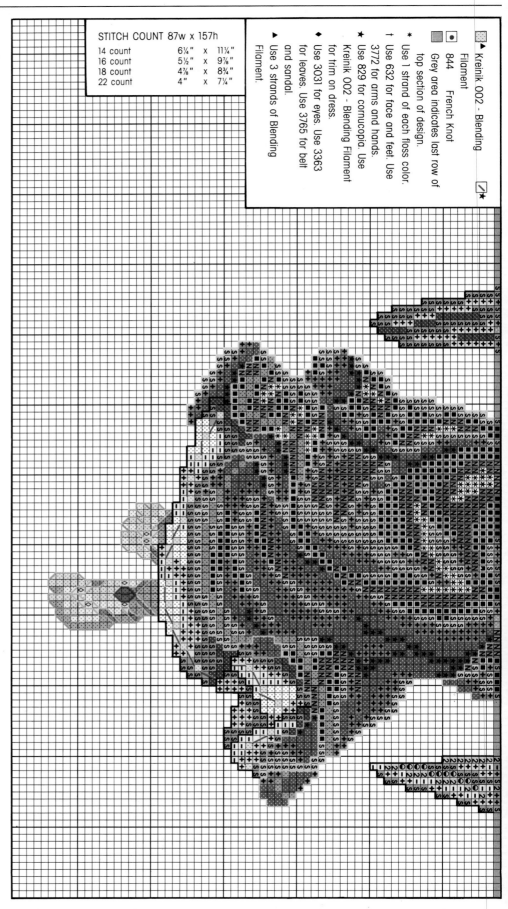

STITCH COUNT 87w x 157h

14 count	6¼"	x	11¼"
16 count	5½"	x	9⅞"
18 count	4⅞"	x	8¾"
22 count	4"	x	7¼"

▶ Kreinik 002 - Blending Filament

● 844   French Knot

Grey area indicates last row of top section of design.

* Use 1 strand of each floss color.

† Use 632 for face and feet. Use 3772 for arms and hands.

★ Use 829 for cornucopia. Use Kreinik 002 - Blending Filament for trim on dress.

◆ Use 3031 for eyes. Use 3363 for leaves. Use 3765 for belt and sandal.

▶ Use 3 strands of Blending Filament.

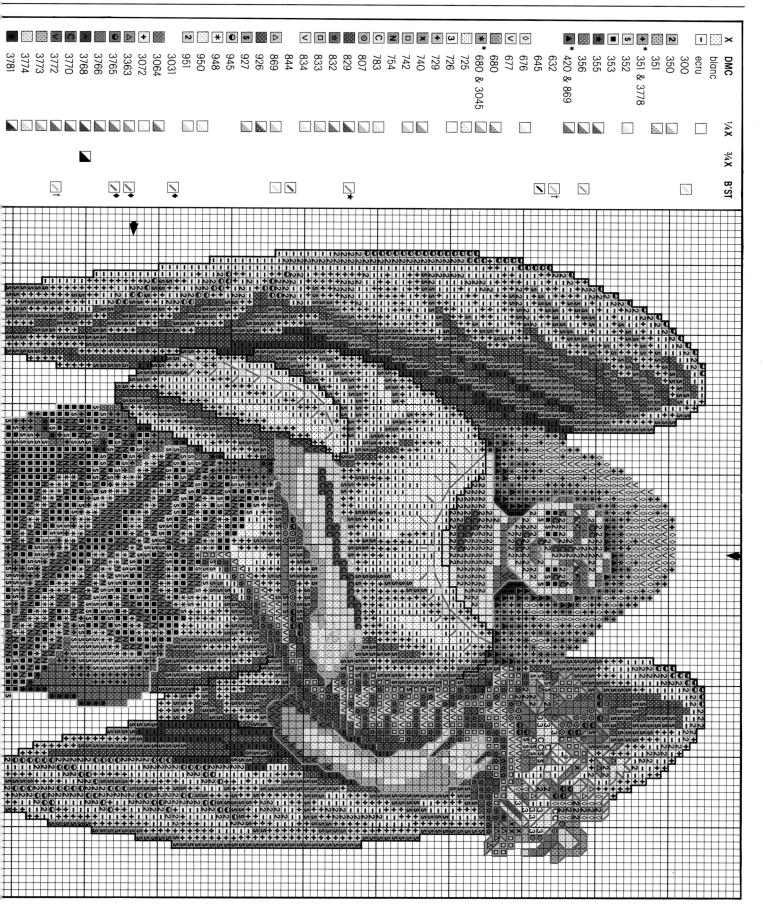

B is for Bells

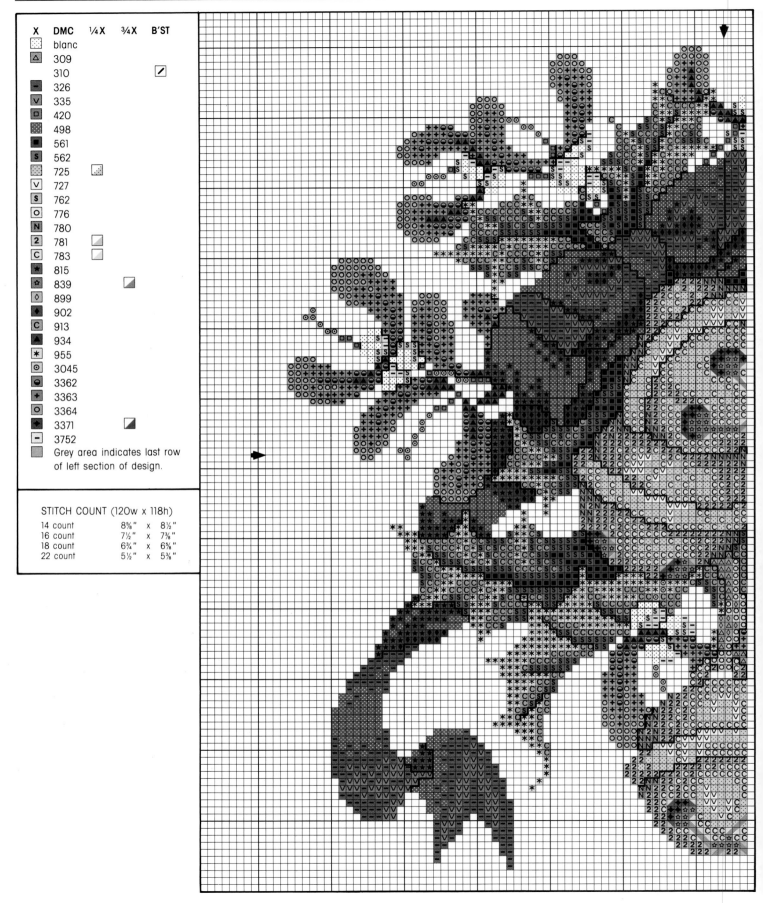

X	DMC	¼X	¾X	B'ST
⁘	blanc			
△	309			
	310			/
–	326			
V	335			
□	420			
⁘	498			
■	561			
S	562			
⁘	725	◩		
V	727			
S	762			
O	776			
N	780			
2	781	◩		
C	783	◩		
★	815			
☆	839		◩	
◊	899			
◆	902			
C	913			
▲	934			
✱	955			
⊙	3045			
⊖	3362			
+	3363			
O	3364			
◆	3371		◩	
–	3752			
▒	Grey area indicates last row of left section of design.			

STITCH COUNT (120w x 118h)

14 count	8⅝"	x	8½"
16 count	7½"	x	7⅜"
18 count	6¾"	x	6⅝"
22 count	5½"	x	5⅜"

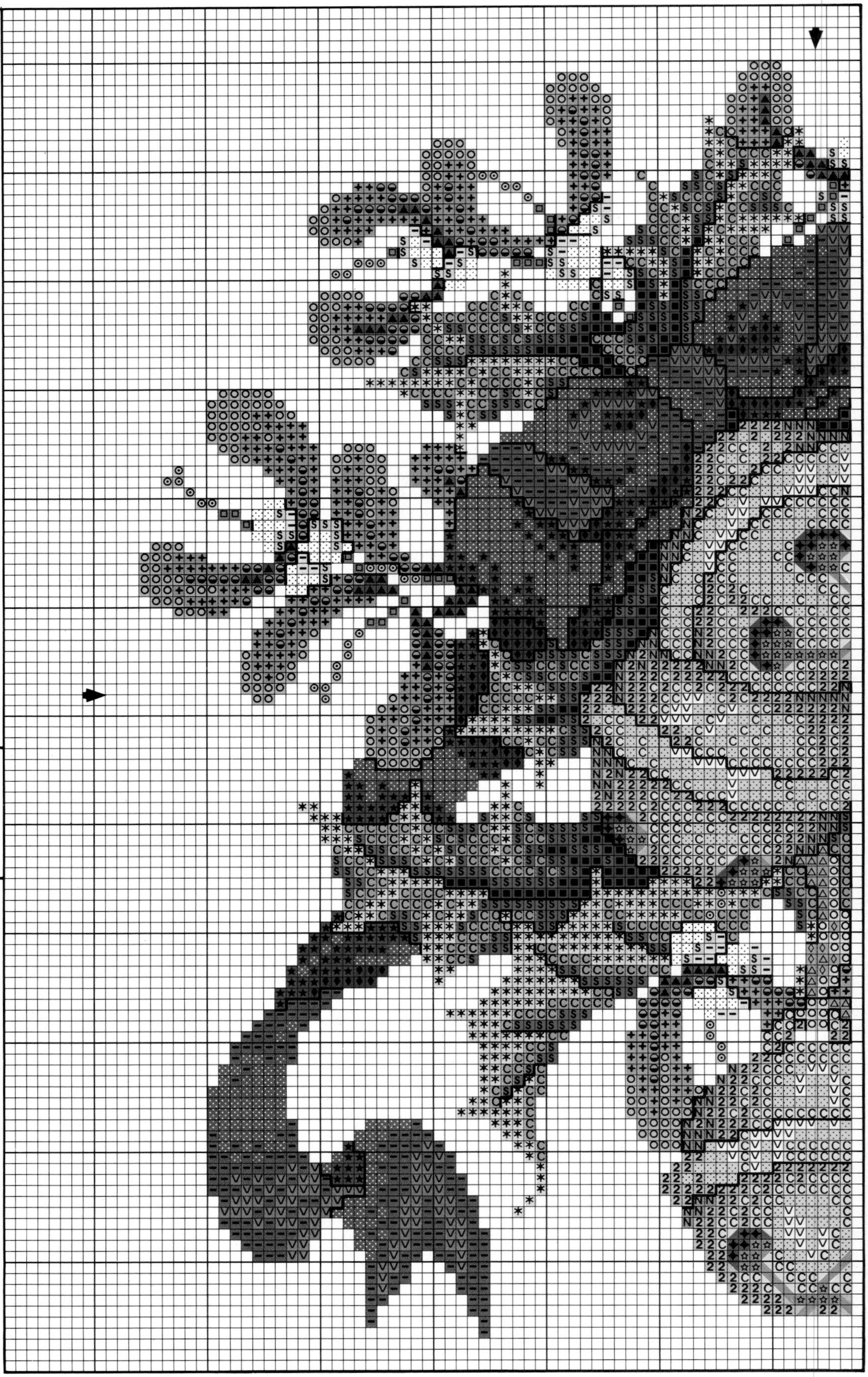

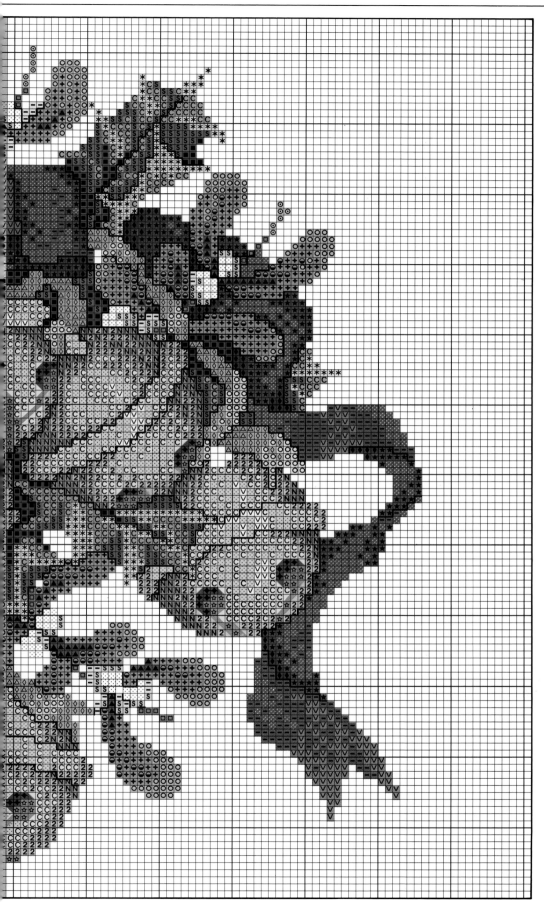

Jingle Bell Afghan (shown on page 9): The design was stitched over 2 fabric threads on an 45" x 58" piece of Midnight Black Anne Cloth (18 ct).

For afghan, cut off selvages of fabric; measure 5½" from raw edge of fabric and pull out 1 fabric thread. Fringe fabric up to missing fabric thread. Repeat for each side. Tie an overhand knot at each corner with 4 horizontal and 4 vertical fabric threads. Working from corners, use 8 fabric threads for each knot until all threads are knotted.

Refer to Diagram for placement of design on fabric; use 6 strands of floss for Cross Stitch and 2 strands for Backstitch.

Designed by Donna Vermillion Giampa.

Diagram

short end of afghan

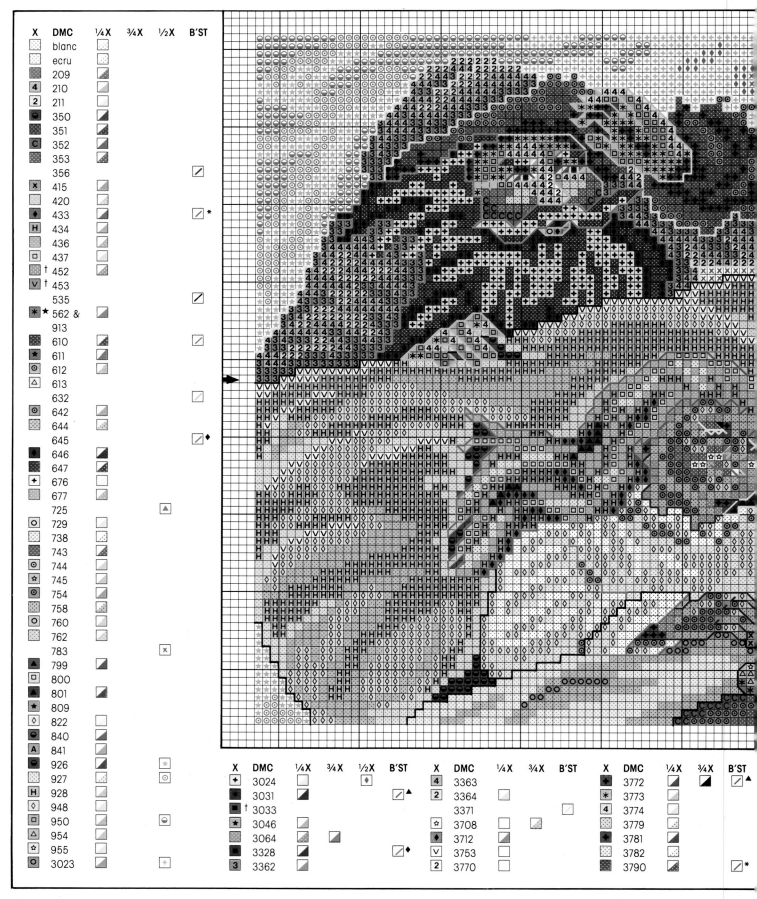

Purple area indicates last row of right section of design.

* Use 433 for girl's hair. Use 3790 for fairies' wings.

† Use 2 strands of floss and 1 strand of Kreinik 032 - Blending Filament.

★ Use 1 strand of each floss color.

◆ Use 3328 for fairies' and girls' mouths. Use 645 for all other.

▲ Use 3031 for Santa's eyes. Use 3772 for fairies' faces and arms.

STITCH COUNT (150w x 89h)

14 count	10¾"	x	6⅜"
16 count	9⅜"	x	5⅝"
18 count	8⅜"	x	5"
22 count	6⅞"	x	4⅛"

Children Dreaming in Frame (shown on page 10): The design was stitched over 2 fabric threads on an 18" x 14" piece of Cream Belfast Linen (32 ct) using 2 strands of floss for Cross Stitch and 1 strand for Half Cross Stitch and Backstitch. It was custom framed.

Needlework adaptation by Nancy Dockter and Carol Emmer.

E is for Evergreens, f is for flowers

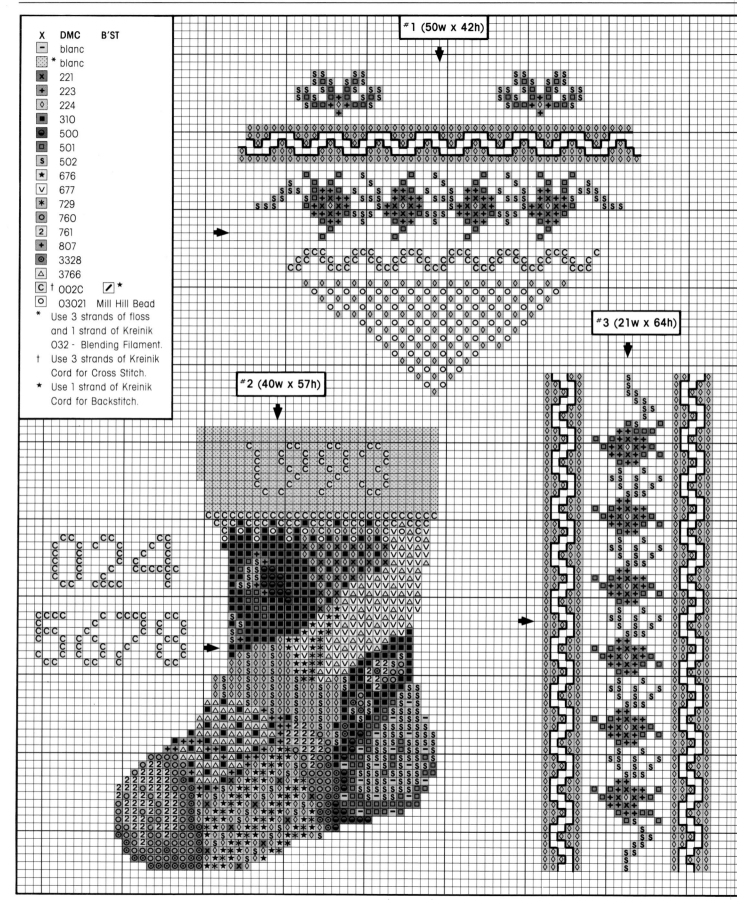

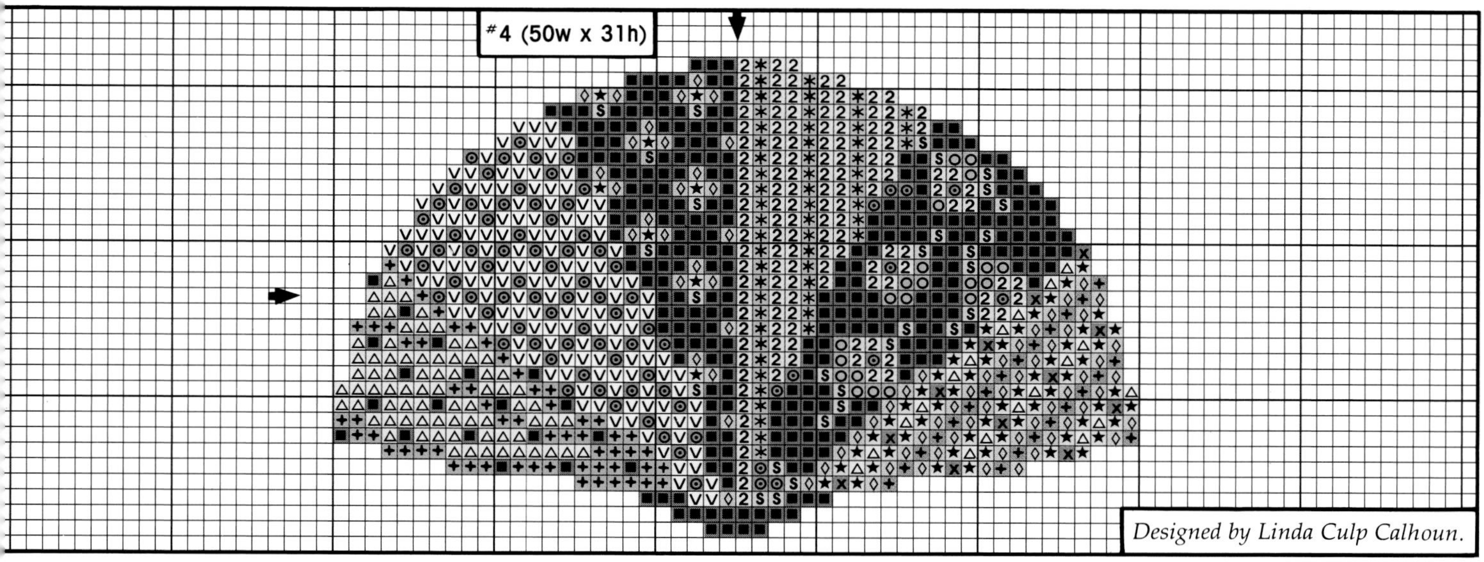
#4 (50w x 31h)
Designed by Linda Culp Calhoun.

art-Shaped Sachet Ornament (shown on page 12): Design #1 was ched on a 7" x 9" piece of Tea Aida (14 ct) using 3 strands of floss Kreinik Cord for Cross Stitch as noted in color key and 1 strand of einik Cord for Backstitch. To attach beads, use 1 strand DMC ecru ibroidery floss and refer to General Instructions, page 95.

For heart sachet, you will need 7" x 9" piece of Aida for backing, ead to match fabric, tracing paper, pencil, 14" length of ¾"w egathered lace, and 16" lengths of various colors of 1/16"w ribbon.

For pattern, fold a piece of tracing paper in half; place fold on shed line of pattern and trace solid lines. Cut out pattern, unfold and ess flat. Matching right sides and raw edges, place backing fabric d stitched piece together. Center pattern on wrong side of stitched ce and pin in place. Cut out and remove pattern.

Matching gathered edge of lace with raw edge of stitched piece, ste lace to right side of stitched piece. Matching right sides and ving an opening for turning, use a ¼" seam allowance to sew ched piece and backing fabric together. Trim point and clip curves. n right side out and stuff with polyester fiberfill. Place a few drops of ented oil on a small amount of polyester fiberfill and insert in middle sachet; whipstitch opening closed.

Align lengths of ribbon and tie in a small bow; trim ends as desired. er to photo and tack bow to heart sachet.

cking Ornament (shown on page 13): Design #2 was stitched on a square of Tea Aida (14 ct) using 3 strands of floss or Kreinik Cord Cross Stitch as noted in color key. To attach beads, use 1 strand IC ecru embroidery floss and refer to General Instructions, page 95.

For stocking, cut a piece of Aida same size as stitched piece for cking. Matching right sides and raw edges, pin stitched piece and cking fabric together. Leaving top edge open, sew pieces together proximately ¼" away from edge of design. Trim excess fabric ving ½" seam allowance. Clip curves, and turn right side out. Press edge of fabric ⅜" to wrong side; whipstitch in place.

For hanger, fold a 5" length of ⅛" dia. gold trim in half. Whipstitch ds to inside of stocking at right seam.

vender Bag Ornament (shown on pages 12-13): Design #3 was ched on a 6" x 16" piece of Tea Aida (14 ct) using 3 strands of floss Cross Stitch and 1 strand of Kreinik Cord for Backstitch.

For lavender bag, you will need a 3" x 9½" piece of tracing paper, ncil, 6" length of ½" w pregathered lace, 6" x 16" piece of Aida for cking, desired number of Mill Hill Glass Pebble Beads - 05147, and " lengths of various widths of desired ribbon and trim.

Matching right sides and raw edges, pin stitched piece and backing oric together. Center tracing paper on wrong side of stitched piece cing one short end of tracing paper 1¼" below bottom of design; in place. Draw around tracing paper; cut out and remove pattern. Leaving top edge open, sew pieces together using a ¼" seam allowance. Trim corners diagonally, and turn right side out. Press top edge of bag ¼" to wrong side. Beginning at back of bag, place gathered edge of lace ¼" inside bag and whipstitch in place. Fill lavender bag ¾ full with potpourri. Tie lengths of ribbon and trim in a bow around bag; trim ends as desired. Thread Glass Pebble Beads randomly on ends of trim; knot ends.

Fan-Shaped Sachet Ornament (shown on page 12): Design #4 was stitched on a 6" square of Tea Aida (14 ct) using 3 strands of floss for Cross Stitch.

For sachet, you will need a 6" square of Aida for backing, thread to match fabric, 2½" tassel, and a 5" length of ⅛"w ribbon for hanger.

Matching right sides and raw edges, place backing fabric and stitched piece together. Leaving an opening for turning and stuffing, sew backing fabric to stitched piece approximately ¼" away from edge of design. Trim curves and turn right side out; stuff with polyester fiberfill. Place a few drops of scented oil on a small amount of polyester fiberfill and insert in middle of sachet; whipstitch opening closed.

Center tassel at bottom of wrong side of sachet; whipstitch in place. Fold ribbon in half; tack ends to wrong side of top center of sachet.

Purse Ornament (shown on page 13): Design #4 was stitched on a 5½" x 8¾" piece of Brown Perforated Paper (14 ct) using 3 strands of floss for Cross Stitch. Centering design horizontally, stitch top of design two squares away from one short edge of perforated paper.

For purse, you will need a 28" length of ⅛"w ribbon, ⅝" button with shank, and DMC 310 embroidery floss.

Trim long edges of perforated paper one square away from design. Trim curved edge of design 1 square away from design. Sew button to right side of perforated paper 2½" from unstitched short edge. Referring to **Fig. 1** for fold lines, fold perforated paper with stitched piece forming flap (right side of stitching will be on outside). Using 6 strands of floss, Blanket Stitch (see Stitch Diagram, page 95) along each side through both layers to form purse. Fill purse with potpourri.

For hanger, cut one 11" length of ribbon; tack ends together to form a circle. Slip ribbon under flap and secure tacked ends to wrong side of stitched piece at fold. For tie, fold remaining length of ribbon in half. Tack fold to wrong side of flap at bottom center. Wrap ends around button and tie in bow. Trim ribbon ends as desired.

Fig. 1

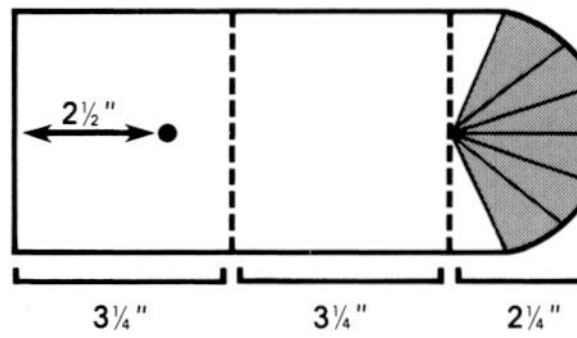
2½"
3¼"
3¼"
2¼"

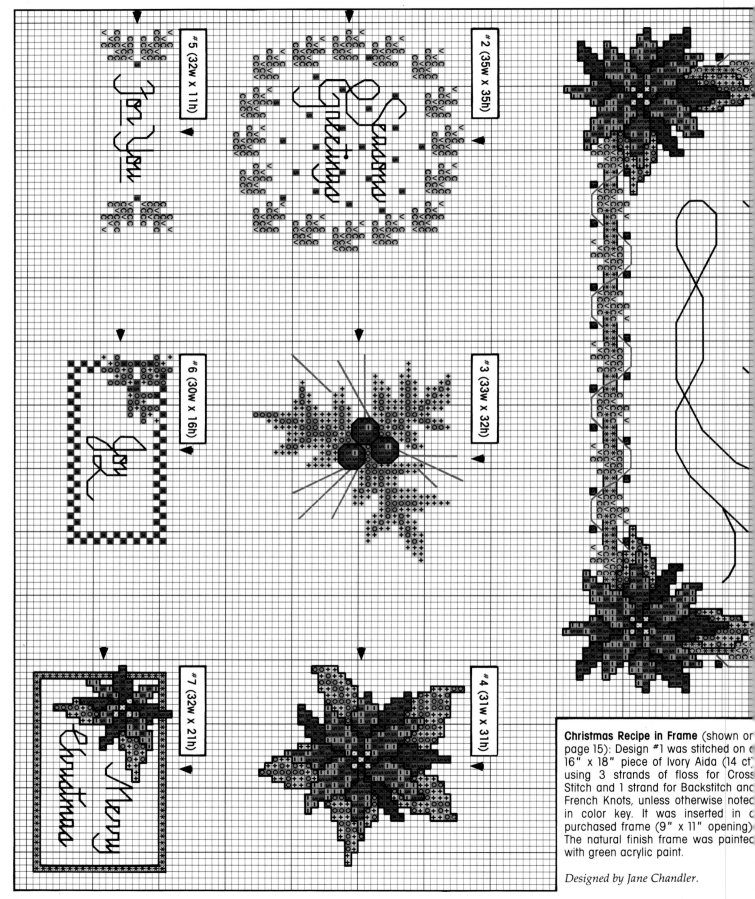

Christmas Recipe in Frame (shown on page 15): Design #1 was stitched on a 16" x 18" piece of Ivory Aida (14 ct) using 3 strands of floss for Cross Stitch and 1 strand for Backstitch and French Knots, unless otherwise noted in color key. It was inserted in a purchased frame (9" x 11" opening). The natural finish frame was painted with green acrylic paint.

Designed by Jane Chandler.

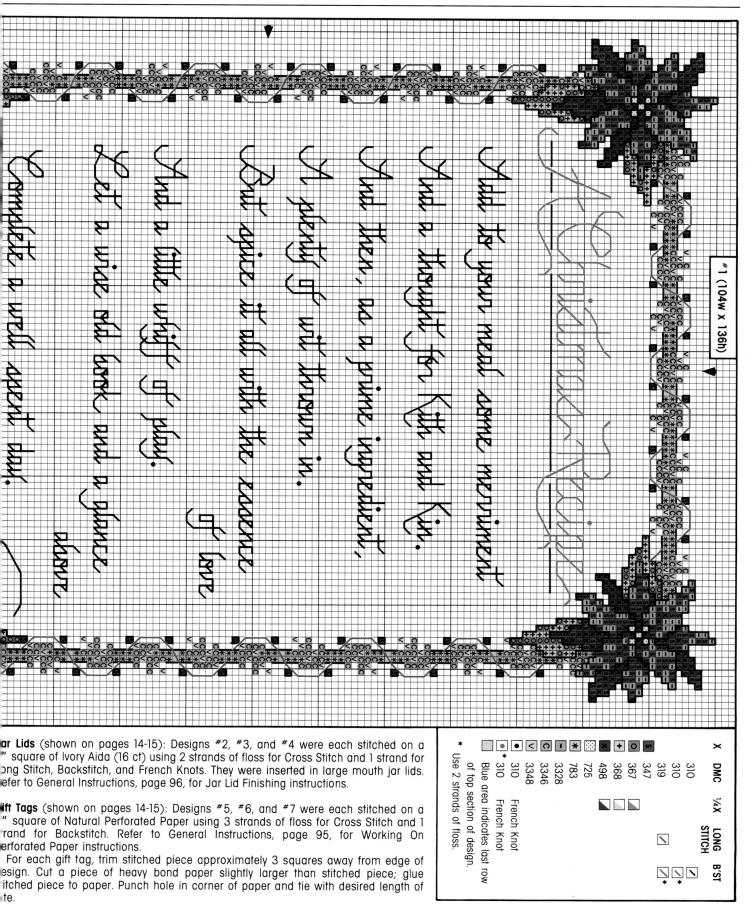

A Christmas Recipe

Add to your meal some merriment

And a thought for Kith and Kin.

And then, as a prime ingredient,

A plenty of will thrown in.

But spice it all with the essence of love

And a little whiff of play.

Let a wise old book and a glance above

Complete a well spent day.

#1 (104w x 136h)

ar Lids (shown on pages 14-15): Designs #2, #3, and #4 were each stitched on a
" square of Ivory Aida (16 ct) using 2 strands of floss for Cross Stitch and 1 strand for
ong Stitch, Backstitch, and French Knots. They were inserted in large mouth jar lids.
efer to General Instructions, page 96, for Jar Lid Finishing instructions.

ift Tags (shown on pages 14-15): Designs #5, #6, and #7 were each stitched on a
" square of Natural Perforated Paper using 3 strands of floss for Cross Stitch and 1
rand for Backstitch. Refer to General Instructions, page 95, for Working On
erforated Paper instructions.

For each gift tag, trim stitched piece approximately 3 squares away from edge of
esign. Cut a piece of heavy bond paper slightly larger than stitched piece; glue
itched piece to paper. Punch hole in corner of paper and tie with desired length of
te.

X	DMC	¼X	LONG STITCH	B'ST
	310			
	310			
	319			✓
	347			
	367			
	368			
	498			
	725			
	783			
	3328			
	3346			
	3348			
•	310	French Knot		
✱	310	French Knot		

Blue area indicates last row
of top section of design.

* Use 2 strands of floss.

X	DMC	¼X	¾X	B'ST
	blanc			
	ecru			
*	319			
	321			
2	367			
x	368			
	433			
+	434			
	435			/
C	606			
	611			/
	632			
V	645			
+	646			
C	647			
☆	648			
*	666			
−	* 754 & 3713			
V	760			
☆	* 760 & 3712			
S	761			
	801			/
	814			/
⊙	816			
	844			/
▲	890			
●	895			
S	905			
V	906			
−	907			
2	930			
+	931			
	945			
	950			
◇	951			
	986			
S	3033			
	3328			
x	3712			/
⊙	* 3712 & 3778			
◆	3750			/
	3772			/
⊙	3773			/
◆	3782			

Blue area indicates last row of left section of design.

* Use 2 strands of each floss color.

STITCH COUNT (128w x 128h)

14 count	9¼"	x	9¼"
16 count	8"	x	8"
18 count	7⅛"	x	7⅛"
22 count	5⅞"	x	5⅞"

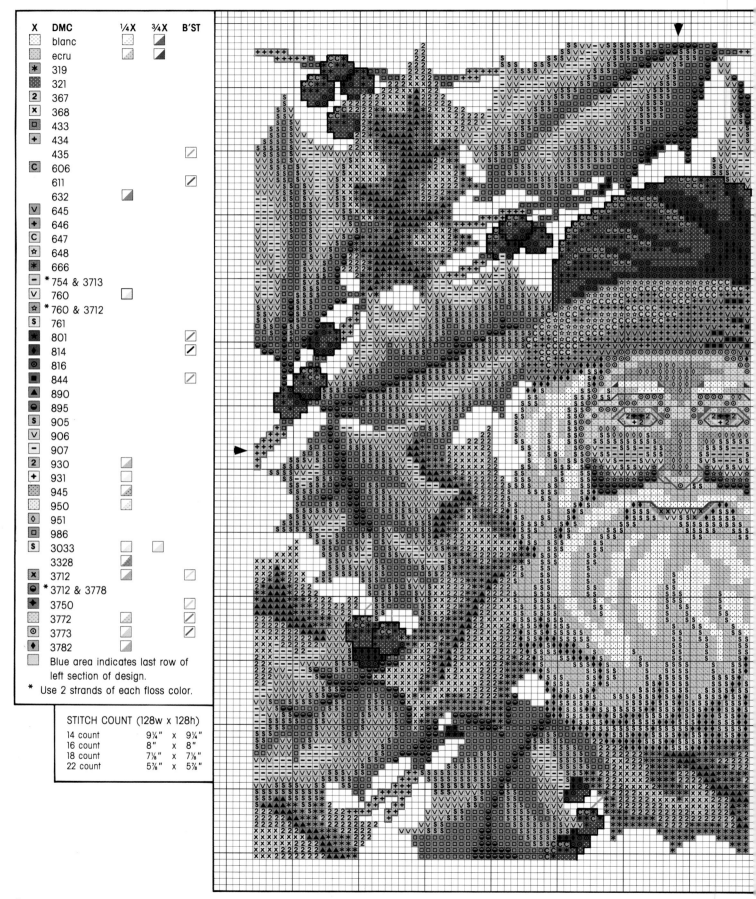

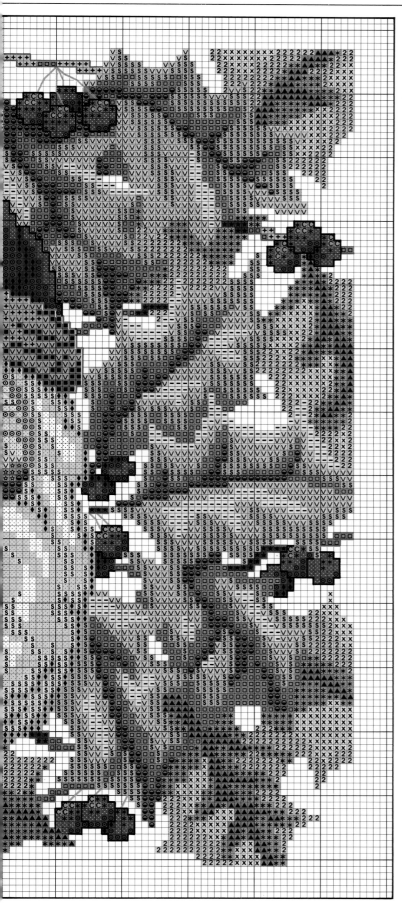

Holly Santa Pillow (shown on page 17): The design was stitched over 2 fabric threads on a 13" square of Black Lugana (25 ct) using 4 strands of floss for Cross Stitch and 1 strand for Backstitch.

For pillow, you will need four 2" x 13" fabric strips for borders, 13" square of Black Lugana for backing fabric, ruler, marking pencil, 54" length of ½" dia. gold cording with attached seam allowance, and polyester fiberfill.

Note: Use ½" seam allowance throughout (unless otherwise noted) and backstitch at beginning and end of each seam.

For pillow front, trim stitched piece ½" larger than design on all sides. For each fabric border, center one fabric strip on one side of stitched piece matching right sides and raw edges. Beginning and ending ½" from each corner of stitched piece, sew fabrics together.

To miter corners, match right sides and short ends of borders and pin borders together at corners. Use a ruler and draw a diagonal line from end of seam to outside corner of borders (**Fig. 1**). This will be stitching line.

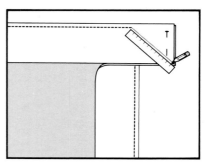

Pin borders together along drawn line, making sure seams on stitched piece match exactly. Sew directly on drawn line; remove pins. Turn mitered corner right side up. Make sure that border seams match; check to see that there is not a gap at the inner end of the seam and that corners do not pucker. Trim seam allowances to ¼" and press seam allowances open.

If needed, trim seam allowance of cording to ½". Start 2" from end of cording; beginning and ending at bottom center of pillow front, baste cording to right side of fabric border making ⅜" clips in seam allowance of cording at each corner. Ends of cording should overlap 4"; turn overlapped ends of cording toward outside edge of pillow front. Baste across overlapped cording as shown in **Fig. 2.**

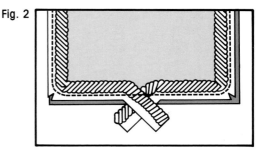

Fig. 2

Matching right sides and raw edges and leaving an opening for turning, use a zipper foot and sew pillow front and backing fabric together; trim seam allowances diagonally at corners. Trim excess cording and turn pillow right side out, carefully pushing corners outward. Stuff pillow with polyester fiberfill and whipstitch opening closed.

Needlework adaptation by Nancy Dockter.

I is for Ice

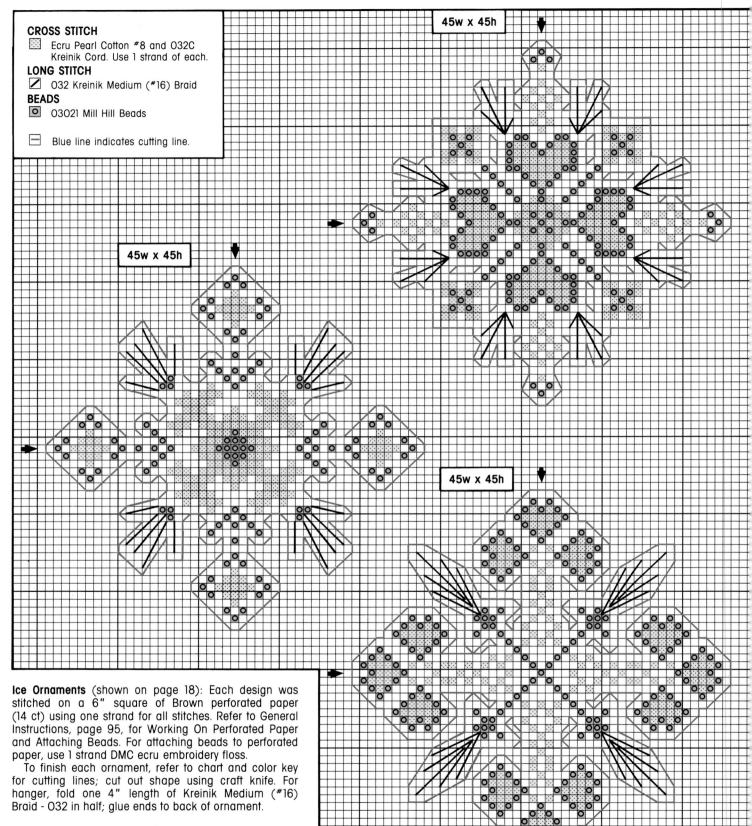

CROSS STITCH
▒ Ecru Pearl Cotton #8 and 032C Kreinik Cord. Use 1 strand of each.

LONG STITCH
◢ 032 Kreinik Medium (#16) Braid

BEADS
◉ 03021 Mill Hill Beads

⊟ Blue line indicates cutting line.

45w x 45h

45w x 45h

45w x 45h

Ice Ornaments (shown on page 18): Each design was stitched on a 6" square of Brown perforated paper (14 ct) using one strand for all stitches. Refer to General Instructions, page 95, for Working On Perforated Paper and Attaching Beads. For attaching beads to perforated paper, use 1 strand DMC ecru embroidery floss.

To finish each ornament, refer to chart and color key for cutting lines; cut out shape using craft knife. For hanger, fold one 4" length of Kreinik Medium (#16) Braid - 032 in half; glue ends to back of ornament.

Designed by Linda Culp Calhoun.

M IS FOR MISTLETOE

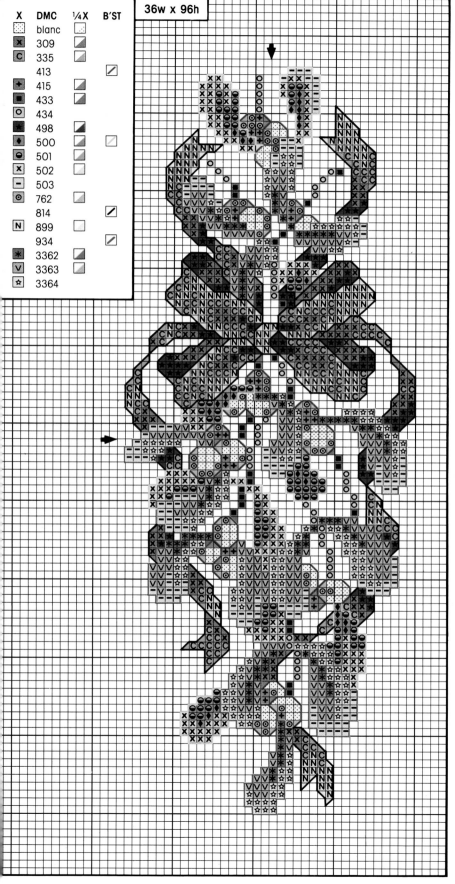

X	DMC	¼X	B'ST
	blanc		
X	309		
C	335		
	413		⟋
✦	415		
■	433		
○	434		
■	498		
◆	500		⟋
◖	501		
X	502		
—	503		
◉	762		
	814		⟋
N	899		
	934		⟋
✱	3362		
V	3363		
☆	3364		

36w x 96h

Mistletoe Kissing Ball (shown on page 24): The design was stitched 3 times separately on 6" x 12" pieces of Tea-Dyed Irish Linen (36 ct). It was stitched over 2 fabric threads using 2 strands of floss for Cross Stitch and 1 strand for Backstitch.

For kissing ball, you will need tracing paper, pencil, fabric marking pencil, craft glue, 5½" dia. Styrofoam® ball, 25mm wooden bead painted gold, small sprig of artificial mistletoe, 12" double tasseled cord, 1½" gold tassel, 12" square of linen, and various trims as desired.

Trace patterns onto tracing paper; cut out patterns. Center Pattern A on right side of each stitched piece and draw around pattern with fabric marking pencil; cut out shapes. Repeat 3 times with Pattern B on 12" square of linen.

Apply glue to **edges only** on wrong side of one stitched piece; smooth and press edges onto ball. Matching points and aligning raw edges, continue gluing fabric pieces around ball alternating stitched pieces and linen pieces. Refer to photo and glue desired trims over raw edges of fabric pieces. Cut 28" lengths of various colors and widths of desired trims; align trims and tie in a bow. Wrap double tasseled cord around center of bow and tie in a knot. Glue top of knotted cord to base of ball; allow to dry. Trim ends to various lengths as desired. Refer to photo to glue mistletoe sprig to base of ball.

For hanger, fold one 10" length of desired trim in half; knot ends together. Thread folded end through wooden bead. Glue top of 1½" gold tassel to base of bead; allow to dry. Find center of tassel and spread open; glue center of tassel to top of ball. Wrap and glue decorative trims around bead as desired.

Designed by Donna Vermillion Giampa.

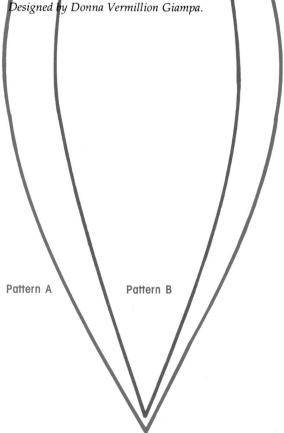

Pattern A   Pattern B

J for the Joy

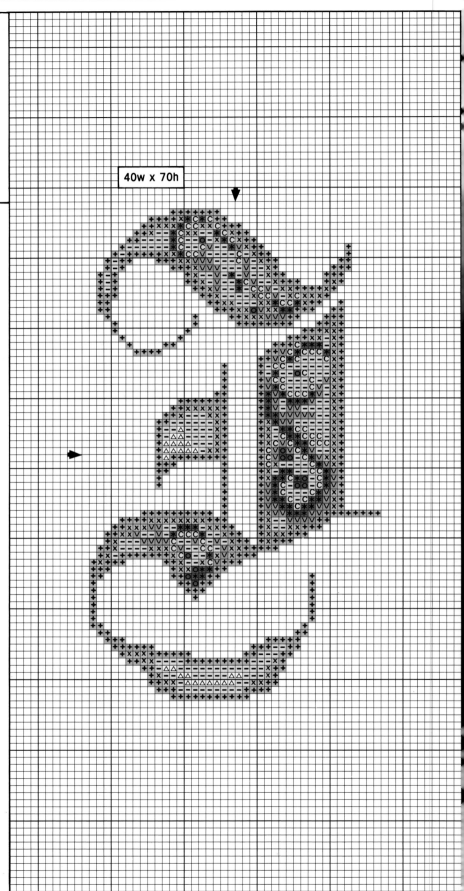

40w x 70h

Joy Bellpull (shown on page 21): The design was stitched over 2 fabric threads on a 16" x 34" piece of Black Lugana (25 ct). Centering letters horizontally, begin stitching with top of "J" design 5" from one short edge of fabric; leave approximately ¾" between letters. Refer to color key for type of thread and number of strands used for Cross Stitch.

For bellpull, you will need tracing paper, pencil, 16" x 34" piece of Lugana for backing, 51" length of purchased ⅛" dia. gold cording with attached seam allowance, 51" length of ⅛" dia. cord, 2" x 51" bias strip of fabric for cording, 7" tassel, 17" length of ¼" dia. gold cord for hanger, bellpull hardware, and various trims as desired.

For pattern, cut one 6¾" x 25½" piece of tracing paper; fold paper in half lengthwise. Referring to **Fig. 1**, measure 3½" from one short end of paper and draw a diagonal line to corner. Cut along drawn line, unfold pattern and press flat. Center pattern on wrong side of stitched piece with point of pattern 3½" below bottom of design; pin in place. Leaving ½" seam allowance on all sides, cut out and remove pattern. Cut backing fabric same size as stitched piece.

Fig. 1

If needed, trim seam allowance of gold cording to ½". Matching right sides and raw edges and beginning at one top corner of stitched piece, use a zipper foot and a ½" seam allowance to baste gold cording to stitched piece; make ⅜" clips in seam allowance of cording at each corner.

For fabric cording, center cord on wrong side of bias strip; matching long edges, fold strip over cord. Use zipper foot to machine baste along length of strip close to cord; trim seam allowance to ⅝". Repeat instructions for gold cording to baste fabric cording in place.

Matching right sides and raw edges and leaving top edge open, use a zipper foot and ½" seam allowance to sew backing fabric to stitched piece. Trim corners diagonally; turn stitched piece right side out. Press top edge ½" to back of bellpull. Fold top edge 1½" to back; whipstitch pressed edge to back of bellpull and insert bellpull hardware. Whipstitch ends of hanger to top corners of wrong side of bellpull, and whipstitch top of tassel to bottom point of bellpull. Refer to photo to trim tassel and hanger as desired.

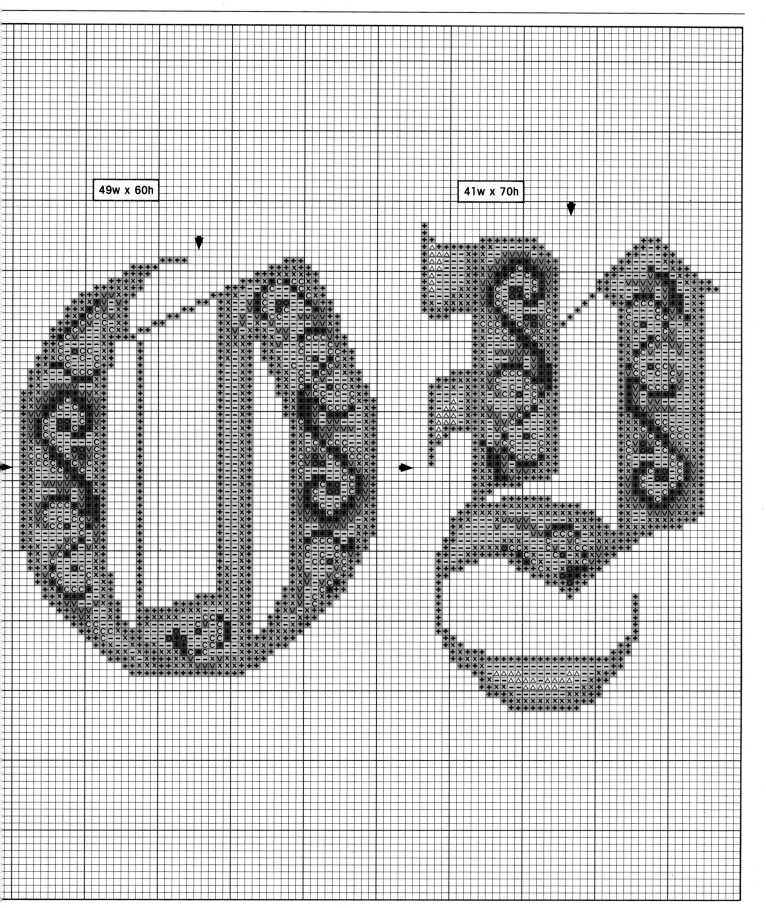

49w x 60h

41w x 70h

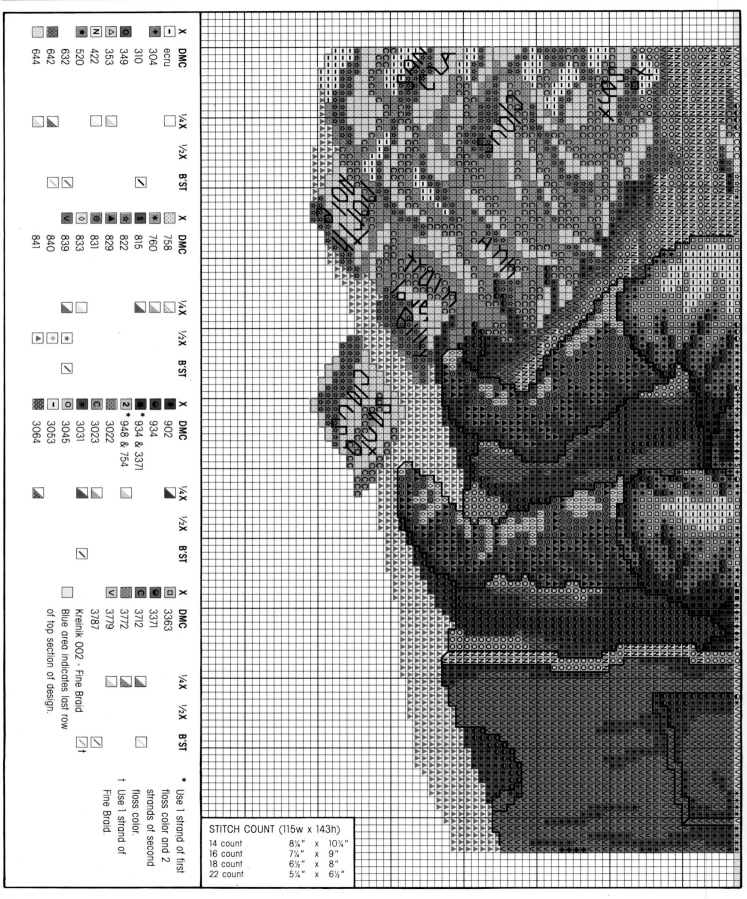

X		DMC
▨	▨	ecru
▨	▨	304
★	N	310
▷	◙	349
⊞	I	353
		422
		520
		632
		642
		644

¼X	½X	B'ST
▨	□	
▨	▨	◹
	▨	
	▨	

X		DMC
▨	★	758
◈	◆	760
◉	S	815
▶		822
◇		829
▨		831
		833
		839
		840
		841

¼X	½X	B'ST
▨	▨	◹
▶	◆	★
	▨	
		◹

X		DMC
▨	◐	902
I	◙	934
O	★	934 & 3371
C	▨	948 & 754 *
◆	2	3022
		3023
		3031
		3045
		3053
		3064

¼X	½X	B'ST
▨	▨	◹
		◹
		◹

X		DMC
□	◐	3363
◙	C	3371
□	◙	3712
▨	C	3772
▨	V	3779
□		3787

¼X	½X	B'ST
□		
	▨ ▨	
◹	◹†	

Kreinik 002 - Fine Braid
Blue area indicates last row
of top section of design.

* Use 1 strand of first
floss color and 2
strands of second
floss color.
† Use 1 strand of
Fine Braid.

STITCH COUNT (115w x 143h)		
14 count	8¼"	x 10¼"
16 count	7¼"	x 9"
18 count	6½"	x 8"
22 count	5¼"	x 6½"

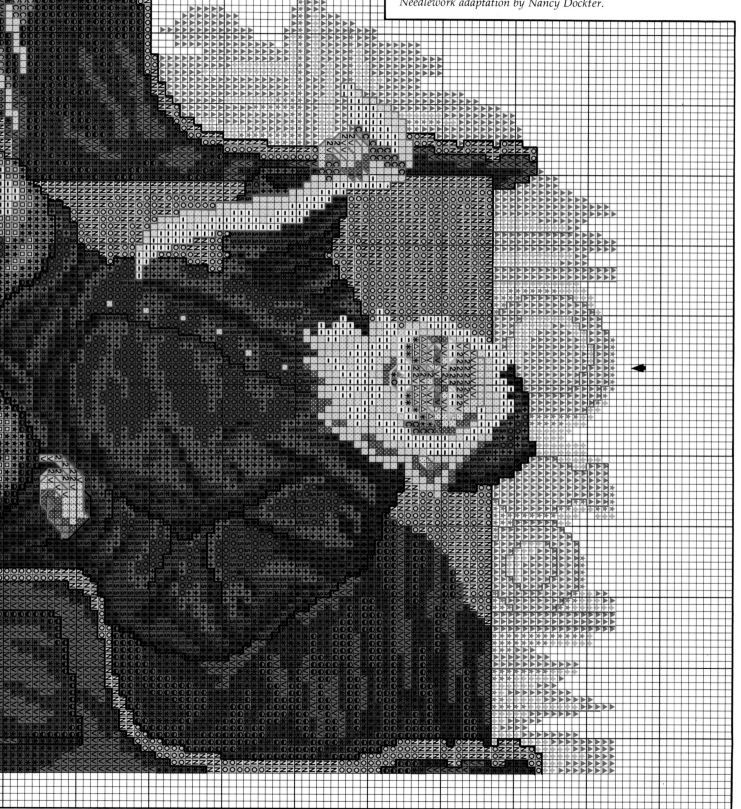

Kriss Kringle Reading Letters in Frame (shown on page 22): The design was stitched over 2 fabric threads on a 16" x 18" piece of Tea-Dyed Irish Linen (32 ct) using 3 strands of floss for Cross Stitch and 1 strand for Half Cross Stitch and Backstitch. It was custom framed.

Needlework adaptation by Nancy Dockter.

n for the night

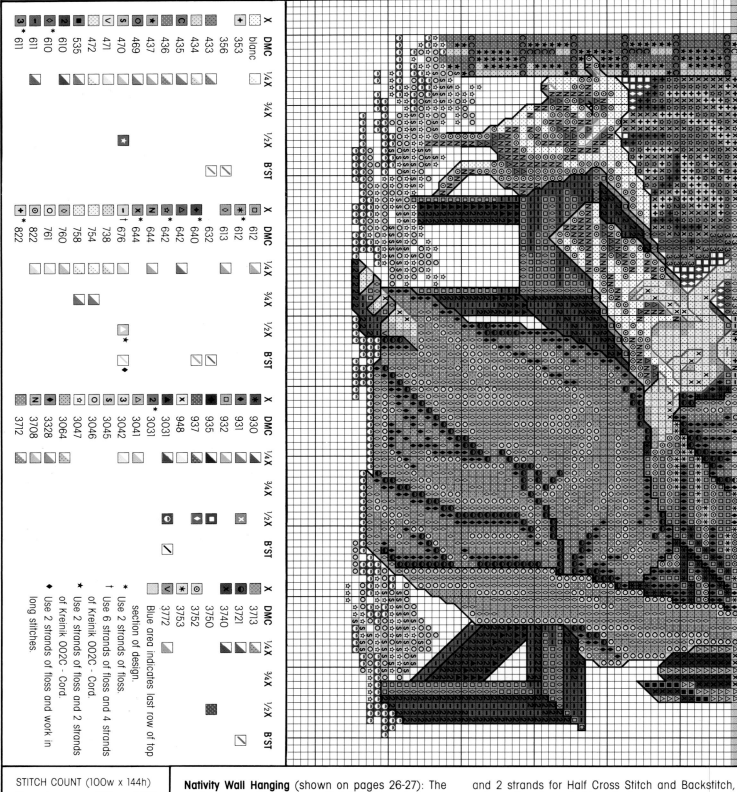

X	¼X	¾X	½X	B'ST	DMC
					blanc
					353
					356
					433
					434
					435
					436
					437
					469
					470
					471
					472
					535
					610
		★			610
					611
					611

X	¼X	¾X	½X	B'ST	DMC
					612
					612
					613
					632
					640
					642
					642
					644
					644
					676
					738
					754
					758
					760
					761
					822
					822

X	¼X	¾X	½X	B'ST	DMC
					930
					931
					932
					935
					937
					948
					3031
					3031
					3041
					3042
					3045
					3046
					3047
					3064
					3328
					3708
					3712

X	¼X	¾X	½X	B'ST	DMC
					3713
					3721
					3740
					3750
					3752
					3753
					3772

Blue area indicates last row of top section of design.

* Use 2 strands of floss.
† Use 6 strands of floss and 4 strands of Kreinik 002C - Cord.
★ Use 2 strands of floss and 2 strands of Kreinik 002C - Cord.
◆ Use 2 strands of floss and work in long stitches.

STITCH COUNT (100w x 144h)

14 count	7¼"	x 10⅜"
16 count	6¼"	x 9"
18 count	5⅝"	x 8"
22 count	4⅝"	x 6⅝"

Nativity Wall Hanging (shown on pages 26-27): The design was stitched over 2 fabric threads on a 21" x 39½" piece of Cracked Wheat Ragusa (14 ct) using six strands of floss for Cross Stitch and 2 strands for Half Cross Stitch and Backstitch, unless otherwise noted in color key.

Center design horizontally and stitch with top of design 7½" from one short edge of fabric. Measure

" from bottom of design and pull out one fabric thread. Fringe up to missing fabric thread. On each long edge turn fabric under ½" and press; turn fabric under ½" again and hem. To finish bottom, start at left side and tie an overhand knot using approximately 8 fabric threads.

Continue across in same manner until all threads are knotted. Trim fringe to 5". For casing at top edge, turn fabric under ½" and press; turn fabric under 2" and hem. Insert stick in casing.

Needlework adaptation by Carol Emmer.

O is for Ornaments

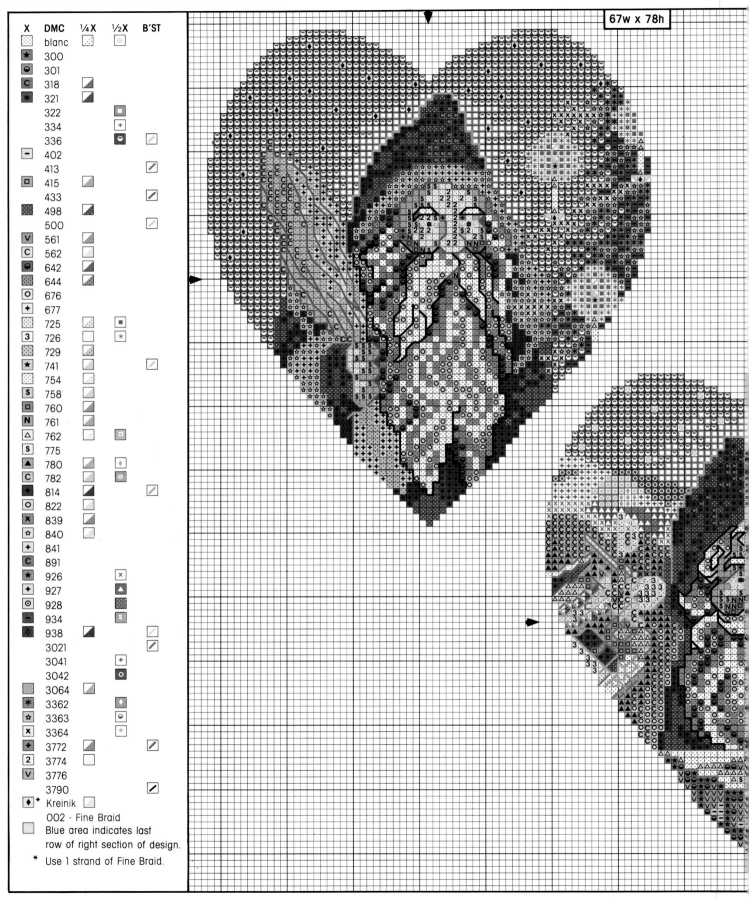

67w x 78h

X	DMC	1/4X	1/2X	B'ST
	blanc			
	300			
	301			
	318			
	321			
	322			
	334			
	336			
	402			
	413			
	415			
	433			
	498			
	500			
	561			
	562			
	642			
	644			
	676			
	677			
	725			
	726			
	729			
	741			
	754			
	758			
	760			
	761			
	762			
	775			
	780			
	782			
	814			
	822			
	839			
	840			
	841			
	891			
	926			
	927			
	928			
	934			
	938			
	3021			
	3041			
	3042			
	3064			
	3362			
	3363			
	3364			
	3772			
	3774			
	3776			
	3790			
	Kreinik			

002 - Fine Braid

Blue area indicates last row of right section of design.

* Use 1 strand of Fine Braid.

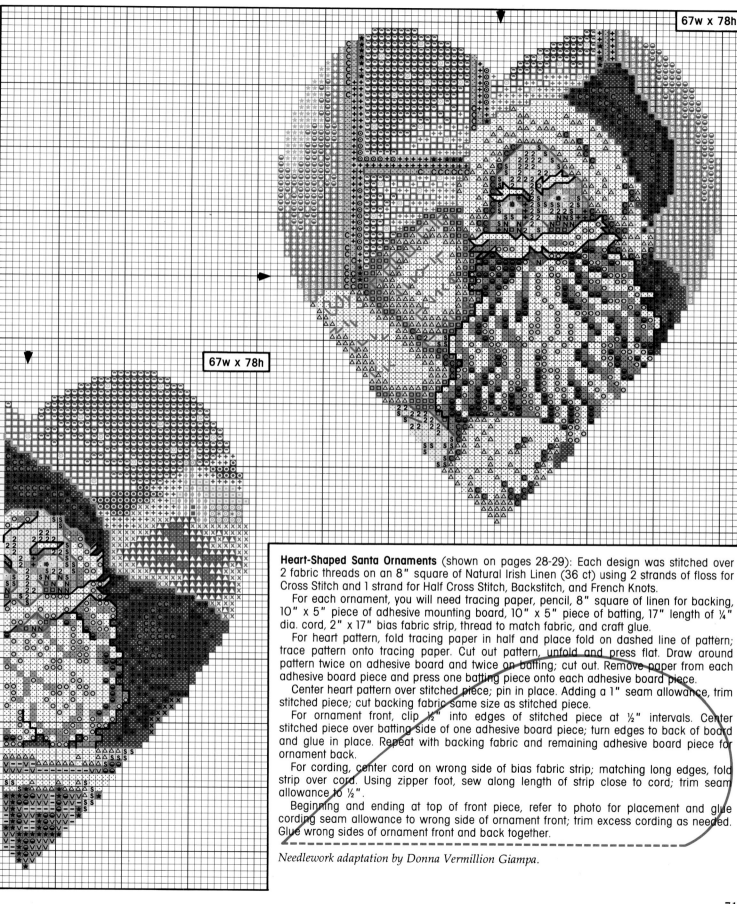

67w x 78h

Heart-Shaped Santa Ornaments (shown on pages 28-29): Each design was stitched over 2 fabric threads on an 8" square of Natural Irish Linen (36 ct) using 2 strands of floss for Cross Stitch and 1 strand for Half Cross Stitch, Backstitch, and French Knots.

For each ornament, you will need tracing paper, pencil, 8" square of linen for backing, 10" x 5" piece of adhesive mounting board, 10" x 5" piece of batting, 17" length of ¼" dia. cord, 2" x 17" bias fabric strip, thread to match fabric, and craft glue.

For heart pattern, fold tracing paper in half and place fold on dashed line of pattern; trace pattern onto tracing paper. Cut out pattern, unfold and press flat. Draw around pattern twice on adhesive board and twice on batting; cut out. Remove paper from each adhesive board piece and press one batting piece onto each adhesive board piece.

Center heart pattern over stitched piece; pin in place. Adding a 1" seam allowance, trim stitched piece; cut backing fabric same size as stitched piece.

For ornament front, clip ½" into edges of stitched piece at ½" intervals. Center stitched piece over batting side of one adhesive board piece; turn edges to back of board and glue in place. Repeat with backing fabric and remaining adhesive board piece for ornament back.

For cording, center cord on wrong side of bias fabric strip; matching long edges, fold strip over cord. Using zipper foot, sew along length of strip close to cord; trim seam allowance to ½".

Beginning and ending at top of front piece, refer to photo for placement and glue cording seam allowance to wrong side of ornament front; trim excess cording as needed. Glue wrong sides of ornament front and back together.

Needlework adaptation by Donna Vermillion Giampa.

p is for peddler

Peddler Advent Calendar (shown on pages 30-31): The design was stitched on a 14" x 26" piece of Antique White Aida (14 ct) using three strands of floss for Cross Stitch and 1 strand for Half Cross Stitch, Backstitch, and French Knots. Center design horizontally and stitch with top of design 4½" from one short edge of fabric.

For calendar, you will need 24 cellophane wrapped candies, fabric glue, ½ yard of craft fleece, ⅞ yard of fabric, thread to match fabric, 2⅛ yards of ⅝"w grosgrain ribbon, 7⅜ yards of ¹⁄₁₆"w satin ribbon, chenille needle, 3¾ yards of jute, green acrylic paint, and 15½" length of ⅝" dia. wooden dowel rod and end caps.

For calendar front, trim stitched piece to measure 11" x 22" with top of design 2½" from top edge. For fabric borders, cut two 3¼" x 11" strips of fabric. Matching right sides and raw edges and using a ½" seam allowance, sew one strip to each short edge of stitched piece. Press seam allowances toward strips. Cut two 3¼" x 26¾" strips of fabric. Matching right sides and raw edges and using a ½" seam allowance, sew one strip to each long edge of stitched piece and attached strips. Press seam allowances toward strips.

For inside ribbon border, cut three 10" lengths of grosgrain ribbon. Glue one length each at top and bottom of stitched piece directly along inside of fabric border. For middle ribbon border, glue ribbon ¾" below bottom of design. Cut two 22" lengths of grosgrain ribbon. Press each short end ½" to wrong side. Glue one length to each long side of stitched piece directly along inside of fabric border.

For candy ties, cut twenty-four 11" lengths of satin ribbon. Refer to photo and lay candies on calendar to determine ribbon placement. For each candy, thread needle with one satin ribbon length and thread through Aida at determined point. Repeat for remaining candies.

For backing, cut a piece of fabric same size as calendar front. Cut a piece of craft fleece same size as backing fabric. Matching right sides and raw edges, place backing fabric on calendar front; place craft fleece on backing fabric. Pin layers together.

Beginning at bottom edge and leaving an opening for turning, use ½" seam allowance and sew all layers together; remove pins. Trim fleece seam allowance close to stitching; trim corners diagonally. Turn right side out, carefully pushing corners outward. Whipstitch opening closed.

For hanging sleeve, cut a 15" x 3" piece of fabric. Press edges ¼" to wrong side; press edges ¼" to wrong side again. Using ¼" seam allowance, sew edges in place. Place long edge of hanging sleeve approximately ¼" below top of wrong side of calendar; pin in place. Whipstitch long edges of hanging sleeve to backing; remove pins.

Paint dowel rod and end caps with paint; allow to dry. Insert dowel rod into hanging sleeve; attach end caps.

For hanger, cut three 44" lengths of jute; aligning lengths, knot at one end and braid lengths together. Tie each end of hanger to ends of dowel rod; trim ends as desired.

Tie each candy in place with ribbon making a bow; trim ends as desired.

Needlework adaptation by Donna Vermillion Giampa

X	DMC	¼X	½X	B'ST
	blanc	■		
	310	■		✔
S	311	■		
	317	■		
C	318	■	✕	
*	319	■		
	320	■		
2	321	■		
✕	322	■		
S	367	■		
△	368	■		
4	415	■	⊙	
★	433	■		
	434	■		
	435	■		
S	436	■		
✕	498	■		
✦	519	■		
	632			✔
	640			✔
	642	■		
✦	644	■		
△	725	■		
☆	727	■		
✕	738	■		
	754	■		
O	758	■		
▲	760	■		
-	761			
	762	■	▲	
★	775	■		
⊖	783	■		
✦	814	■		
3	819	■		
⊙	822	■		
	838	■		
	839	■		
C	840	■		
	841	■		
2	842	■		
	892	■		
★	894	■		
✦	948	■		
*	3032	■		
V	3033	■		
*	3326	■		
	3371			✔
◇	3689	■		
☆	3755	■		
V	3761	■		
▲	3778	■		
2	3781	■		
	3782	■		
●	310	French Knot		

STITCH COUNT (91w x 113h)

14 count	6½"	x	8⅛"
16 count	5¾"	x	7⅛"
18 count	5⅛"	x	6⅜"
22 count	4¼"	x	5¼"

q the Quadrille

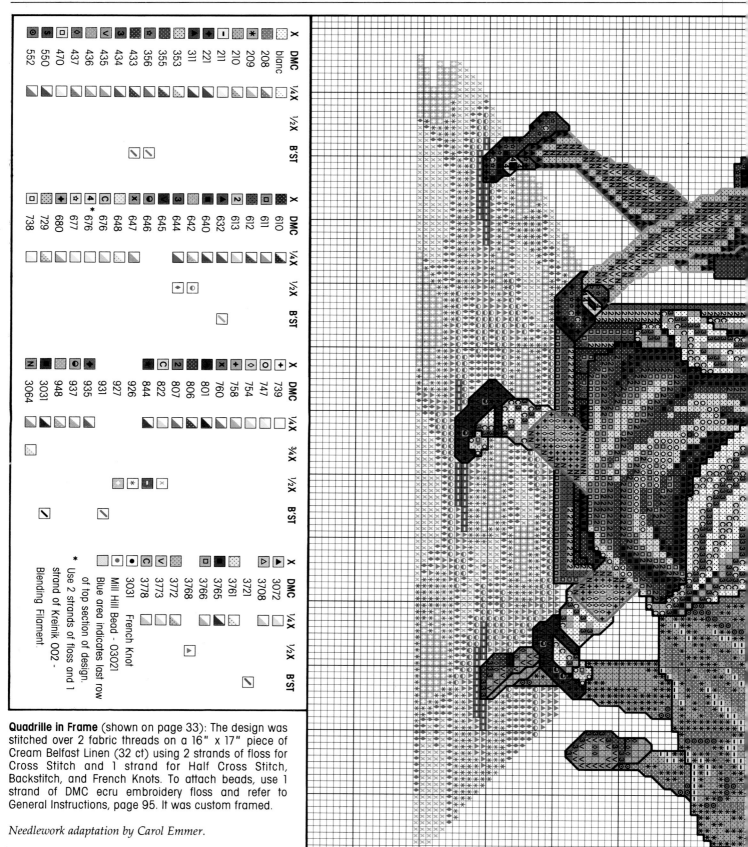

Quadrille in Frame (shown on page 33): The design was stitched over 2 fabric threads on a 16" x 17" piece of Cream Belfast Linen (32 ct) using 2 strands of floss for Cross Stitch and 1 strand for Half Cross Stitch, Backstitch, and French Knots. To attach beads, use 1 strand of DMC ecru embroidery floss and refer to General Instructions, page 95. It was custom framed.

Needlework adaptation by Carol Emmer.

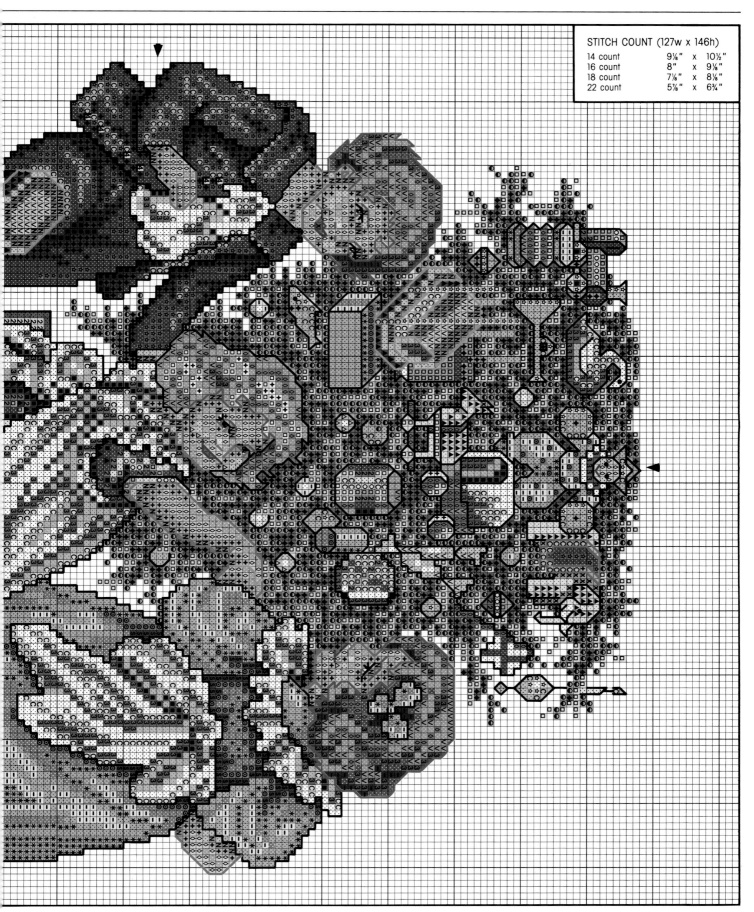

STITCH COUNT (127w x 146h)

count			
14 count	9⅛"	x	10½"
16 count	8"	x	9⅛"
18 count	7⅛"	x	8⅛"
22 count	5⅞"	x	6¾"

Santa and Reindeer Standing Figures (shown on pages 34-35, Reindeer charts on pages 78-79): Each design was stitched on Dirty Aida (14 ct) using three strands of floss for Cross Stitch and 1 strand for Half Cross Stitch, Backstitch, and French Knots, unless otherwise noted in color key.

Refer to photo for placement of 6mm jingle bells. Attach bells using 1 strand DMC 469 embroidery floss.

For each stuffed figure, cut a piece of Aida same size as stitched piece for backing. Matching right sides and raw edges and leaving bottom edge open, sew stitched piece and backing together 2 squares from design as shown in **Fig. 1**. Leaving a ¼" seam allowance, cut out figure. Clip seam allowances at curves; turn figure right side out and carefully push curves outward. Trim bottom edges of figure ½" from bottom of design. Press raw edges ¼" to wrong side; stuff figure with polyester fiberfill up to 1½" from opening.

Fig. 1

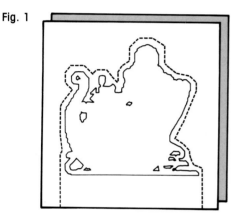

For base, set figure on tracing paper and draw around base of figure. Add a ½" seam allowance to pattern; cut out. Place pattern on a piece of Aida. Use fabric marking pencil to draw around pattern; cut out along drawn line. Baste around base piece ½" from raw edge; press raw edges to wrong side along basting line.

To weight bottom of figure, fill a plastic sandwich bag with a small amount of aquarium gravel. Place bag of gravel into opening of figure.

Pin wrong side of base piece over opening. Whipstitch in place, adding polyester fiberfill as necessary to fill bottom of figure. Remove basting thread.

Using ¹⁄₁₆" dia. gold cord for reins, refer to photo for placement and tack in place.

Designed by Carol Emmer.

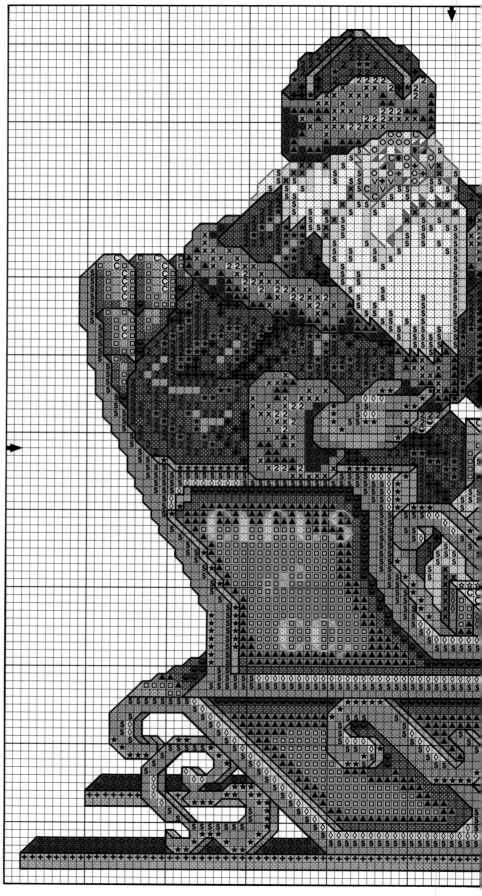

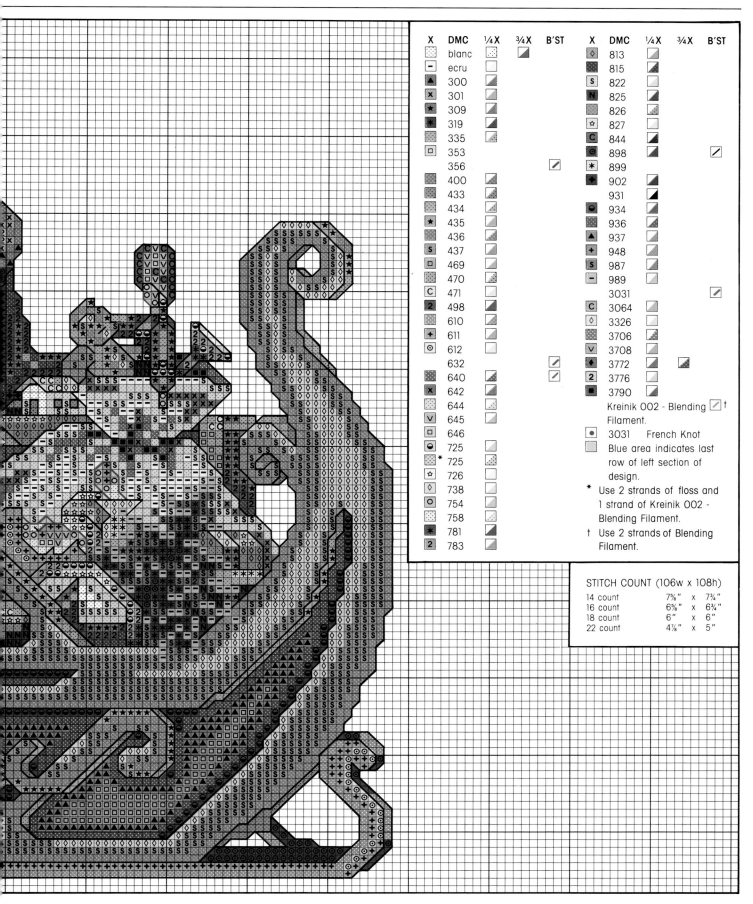

X	DMC	¼X	¾X	B'ST
▒	blanc	■	■	
-	ecru	■		
▲	300	■		
×	301	■		
★	309	■		
✱	319	■		
▒	335	■		
□	353			
	356			■
▒	400	■		
▒	433	■		
▒	434	■		
★	435	■		
▒	436	■		
S	437	■		
□	469	■		
▒	470	■		
C	471	■		
2	498	■		
▒	610	■		
+	611	■		
⊙	612	■		
	632			■
▒	640	■		■
×	642	■		
▒	644	■		
V	645	■		
□	646			
◒	725	■		
▒ *	725	■		
☆	726	■		
◇	738	■		
○	754	■		
▒	758	■		
✱	781	■		
2	783	■		

X	DMC	¼X	¾X	B'ST
◇	813	■		
▒	815	■		
S	822	■		
N	825	■		
▒	826	■		
☆	827	■		
C	844	■		
◎	898	■		■
✱	899			
◆	902	■		
	931	■		
◒	934	■		
▒	936	■		
▲	937	■		
+	948	■		
S	987	■		
-	989	■		
	3031			■
C	3064	■		
◇	3326	■		
▒	3706	■		
V	3708	■		
◆	3772	■	■	
2	3776	■		
■	3790	■		

Kreinik 002 - Blending Filament. ■ †

• 3031 French Knot

▒ Blue area indicates last row of left section of design.

* Use 2 strands of floss and 1 strand of Kreinik 002 - Blending Filament.

† Use 2 strands of Blending Filament.

STITCH COUNT (106w x 108h)

14 count	7⅝"	x	7¾"
16 count	6⅝"	x	6¾"
18 count	6"	x	6"
22 count	4⅞"	x	5"

R for the Reindeer

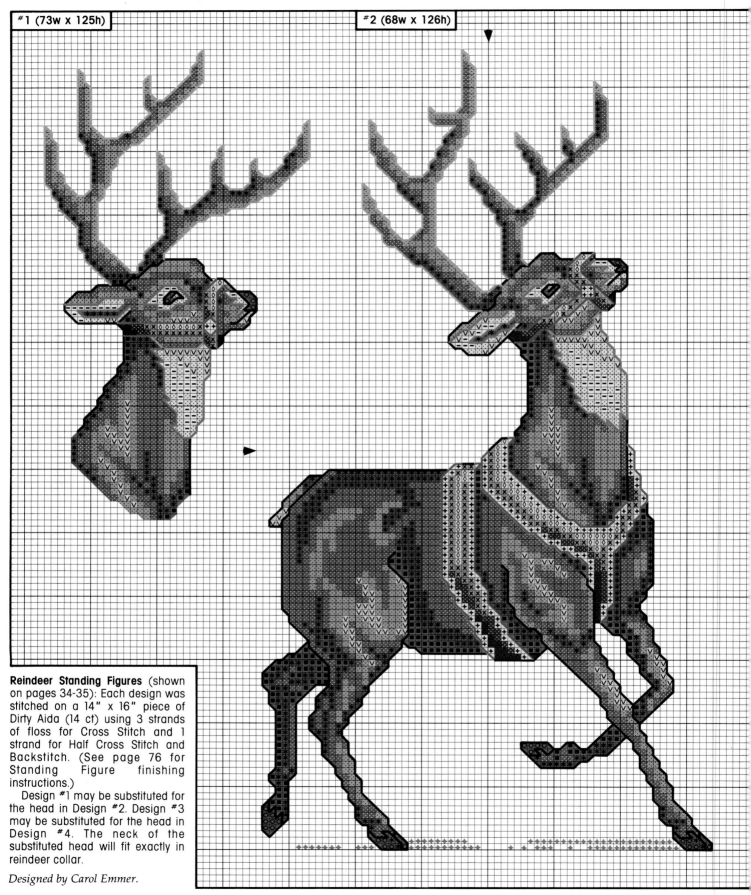

#1 (73w x 125h)

#2 (68w x 126h)

Reindeer Standing Figures (shown on pages 34-35): Each design was stitched on a 14" x 16" piece of Dirty Aida (14 ct) using 3 strands of floss for Cross Stitch and 1 strand for Half Cross Stitch and Backstitch. (See page 76 for Standing Figure finishing instructions.)

Design #1 may be substituted for the head in Design #2. Design #3 may be substituted for the head in Design #4. The neck of the substituted head will fit exactly in reindeer collar.

Designed by Carol Emmer.

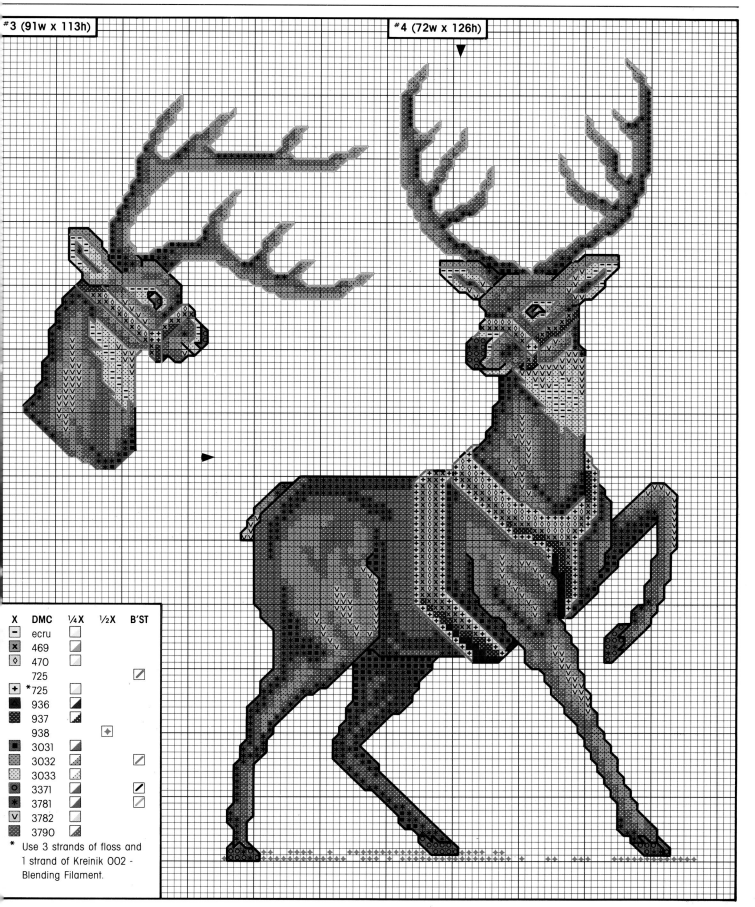

#3 (91w x 113h)   #4 (72w x 126h)

X	DMC	¼X	½X	B'ST
−	ecru			
X	469			
◇	470			
	725			/
+	*725			
■	936			
▨	937			
	938		◆	
▪	3031			
▨	3032			/
▨	3033			
⊙	3371			/
✱	3781			/
V	3782			
▨	3790			

* Use 3 strands of floss and
1 strand of Kreinik 002 -
Blending Filament.

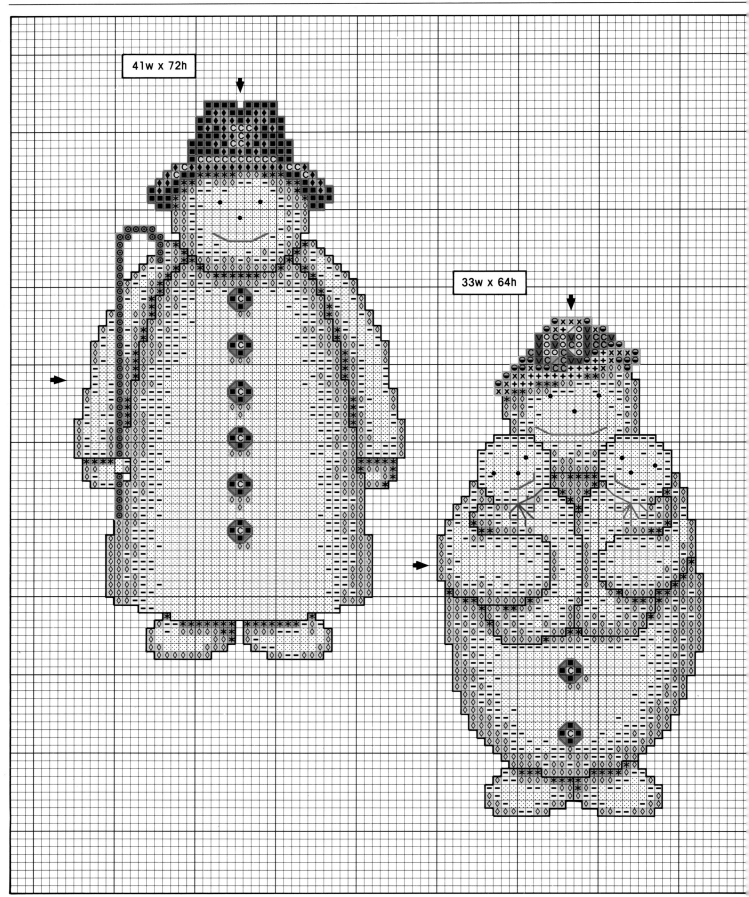

41w x 72h

33w x 64h

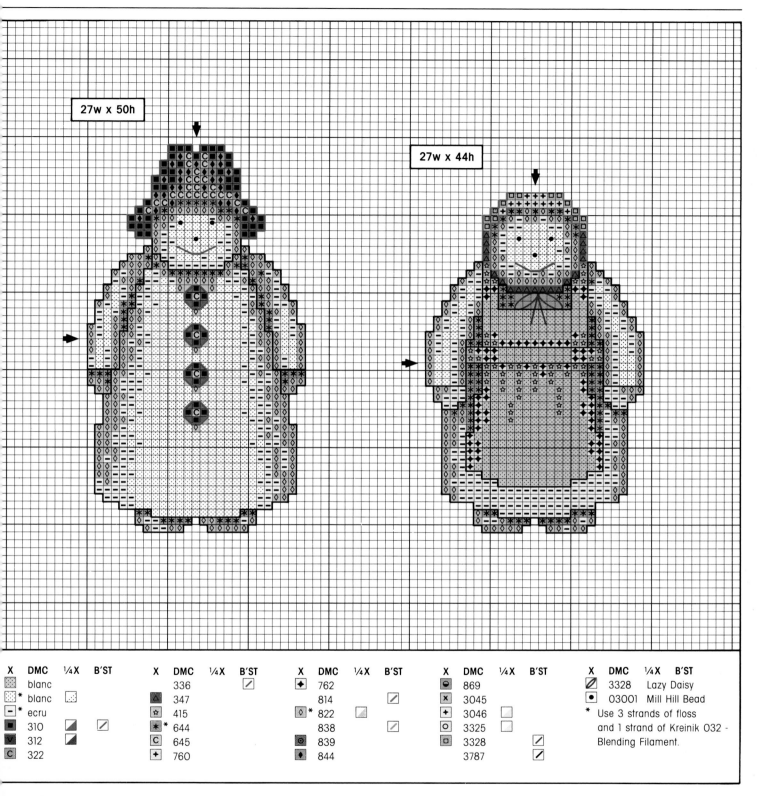

X	DMC	¼X	B'ST		X	DMC	¼X	B'ST		X	DMC	¼X	B'ST		X	DMC	¼X	B'ST		X	DMC	¼X	B'ST		X	DMC	¼X	B'ST
	blanc					336		✓		◆	762				◒	869				⊘	3328		Lazy Daisy
*	blanc				▲	347					814		✓		✕	3045				●	03001		Mill Hill Bead
- *	ecru				☆	415				◇ *	822	◪	✓		+	3046				*	Use 3 strands of floss
■	310	◪	✓		* *	644					838		✓		○	3325					and 1 strand of Kreinik 032 -
V	312	◪			C	645				◎	839				▢	3328		✓			Blending Filament.
C	322				+	760				◆	844					3787		✓			

ow Family Stuffed Shapes (shown on pages 36-37): Each design was tched on a 7" x 9" piece of Dirty Aida (14 ct) using 3 strands of floss Cross Stitch and 1 strand for Backstitch and Lazy Daisy Stitches. To ach beads, use 1 strand DMC 310 embroidery floss.

For each stuffed shape, cut a piece of Aida same size as stitched ce for backing. Matching right sides and raw edges, pin stitched ce and backing fabric together. Leaving an opening for turning and stuffing, sew pieces together ¼" away from edge of design. Trim excess fabric leaving ¼" seam allowance. Trim corners diagonally, clip curves, and turn right side out. Stuff shape with polyester fiberfill and whipstitch opening closed.

Needlework adaptation by Jane Chandler.

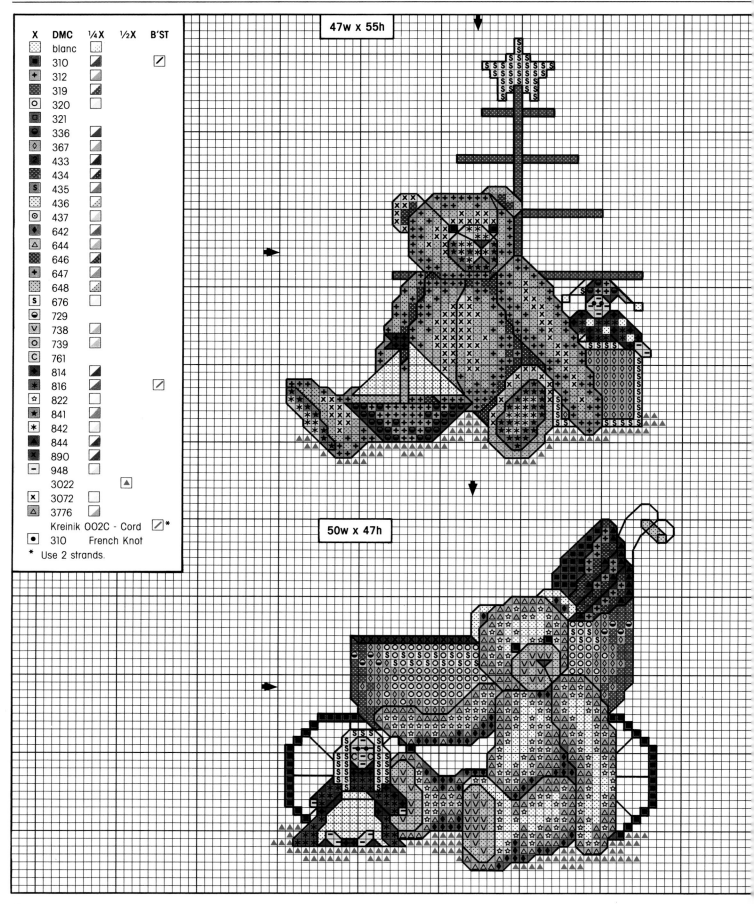

X	DMC	1/4 X	1/2 X	B'ST
	blanc			
	310			
	312			
	319			
	320			
	321			
	336			
	367			
	433			
	434			
	435			
	436			
	437			
	642			
	644			
	646			
	647			
	648			
	676			
	729			
	738			
	739			
	761			
	814			
	816			
	822			
	841			
	842			
	844			
	890			
	948			
	3022			
	3072			
	3776			
	Kreinik 002C - Cord			*
	310	French Knot		
*	Use 2 strands.			

47w x 55h

50w x 47h

ddy Stockings (shown on pages 38-39): Each design was stitched ~~er 2 fabric threads on an 8" x 10" piece of Tea-Dyed Irish Linen~~ '8 ct) using 3 strands of floss for Cross Stitch and 1 strand for Half ross Stitch, Backstitch, and French Knots.

For each stocking, you will need 8" x 10" piece of Tea-Dyed Irish nen for backing, two 8" x 10" pieces of cream fabric for lining, ¼" x 4¼" piece of coordinating fabric for cuff, and 5" length of " w ribbon for hanger

Trace stocking pattern onto tracing paper; cut out pattern. Refer to noto to position pattern on wrong side of stitched piece; pin pattern in ace. Use fabric marking pencil to draw around pattern; remove attern. Matching right sides and raw edges, pin stitched piece and acking fabric together.

Leaving top edge open, sew stocking pieces together directly on own line; remove pins. Trim top edge along drawn line. Trim seam owance to ¼" and clip curves; turn stocking right side out.

Repeat to draw around pattern and sew lining pieces together just side drawn line. Trim top edge along drawn line. Trim seam owance close to stitching. **Do not turn lining right side out**. Press top ge of lining ½" to wrong side.

Matching right side and short edges, fold cuff fabric in half. Using a ' seam allowance, sew short edges together. Matching wrong side and long edges, fold in half and press.

Matching raw edges, place cuff inside stocking with cuff seam at center back of stocking. Use a ½" seam allowance to sew stocking and cuff together. Fold cuff 1½" over stocking and press.

For hanger, fold ribbon in half matching short edges and whipstitch ends to inside of stocking at right seam. With wrong sides facing, place lining inside stocking; whipstitch lining to stocking.

For fabric stockings, substitute desired fabric for linen.

Stiffened Bears: The top portion of each bear (refer to photo) was stitched on a 6" x 7" piece of Ivory Aida (14 ct) using 3 strands of floss for Cross Stitch and 1 strand for Backstitch. They were stiffened and inserted in fabric stockings.

For each stiffened design, you will need fabric stiffener, small foam brush, and 6" x 7" piece of cream medium weight fabric for backing. Apply a heavy coat of fabric stiffener to back of stitched piece using foam brush. Matching wrong sides, place stitched piece on backing fabric, smoothing stitched piece while pressing fabric pieces together; allow to dry. Apply fabric stiffener to backing fabric and allow to dry. Leaving approximately 1" of fabric below bear to insert in stocking, cut out close to edges of stitched design.

Designed by Jane Chandler.

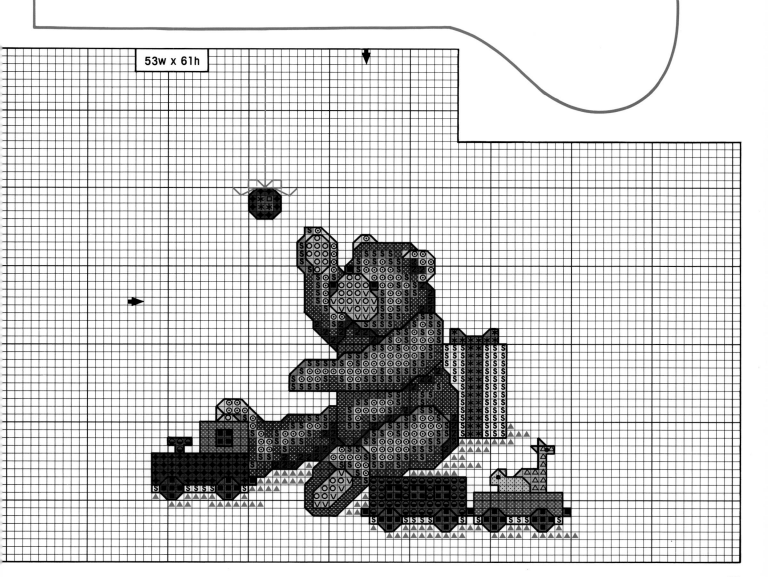

53w x 61h

U is for Uproar

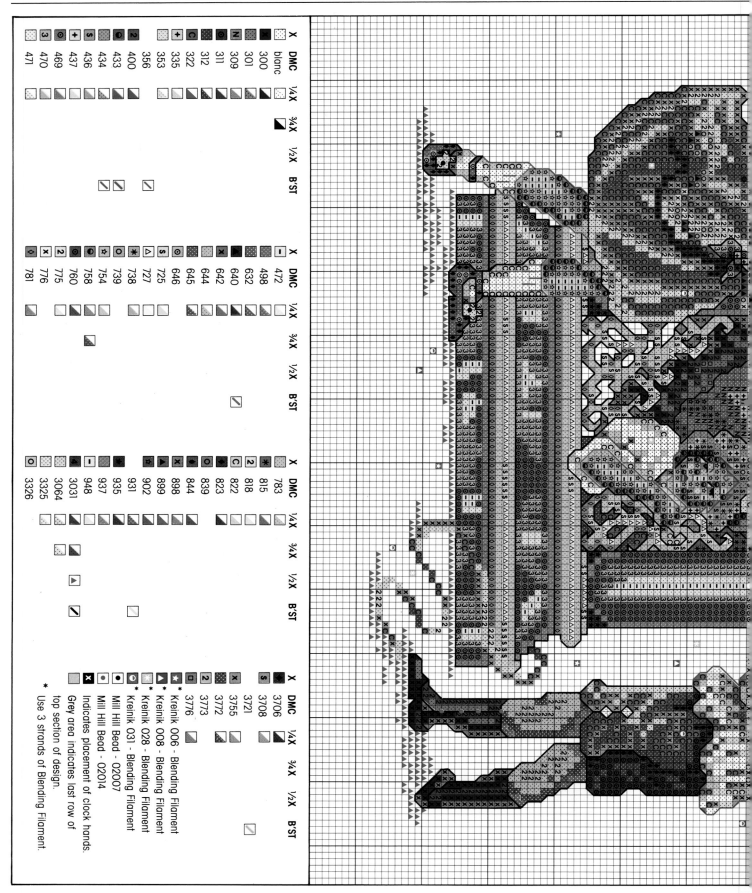

X	DMC	1/4X	3/4X	1/2X	B'ST
	blanc				
	300				
	301				
	309				
	311				
	312				
	322				
	335				
	353				
	356				
	400				
	433				
	434				
	436				
	437				
	469				
	470				
	471				

X	DMC	1/4X	3/4X	1/2X	B'ST
	472				
	498				
	632				
	640				
	642				
	644				
	645				
	646				
	725				
	727				
	738				
	739				
	754				
	758				
	760				
	775				
	776				
	781				

X	DMC	1/4X	3/4X	1/2X	B'ST
	783				
	815				
	818				
	822				
	823				
	839				
	844				
	898				
	899				
	902				
	931				
	935				
	937				
	948				
	3031				
	3064				
	3325				
	3326				

X	DMC	1/4X	3/4X	1/2X	B'ST
	3376				
	3373				
	3772				
	3755				
	3721				
	3708				
	3706				
	Kreinik 006 - Blending Filament				
	Kreinik 008 - Blending Filament				
	Kreinik 028 - Blending Filament				
	Kreinik 031 - Blending Filament				
	Mill Hill Bead - 02007				
	Mill Hill Bead - 02014				

Grey area indicates last row of top section of design.

Indicates placement of clock hands.

* Use 3 strands of Blending Filament.

Uproar Clock (shown on pages 40-41): The design was stitched over 2 fabric threads on an 18" x 21" piece of Ivory Lugana (25 ct) using 3 strands of floss or Kreinik Blending Filament for Cross Stitch as noted in color key, and 1 strand of floss for Half Cross Stitch and Backstitch. To attach beads, use nylon thread and refer to General Instructions, page 95. It was custom framed using ¾" deep molding to accommodate clock movement. Refer to manufacturer's instructions to add clock movement for ¼" thick clock face to framed piece (hands placement indicated on chart).

Designed by Carol Emmer.

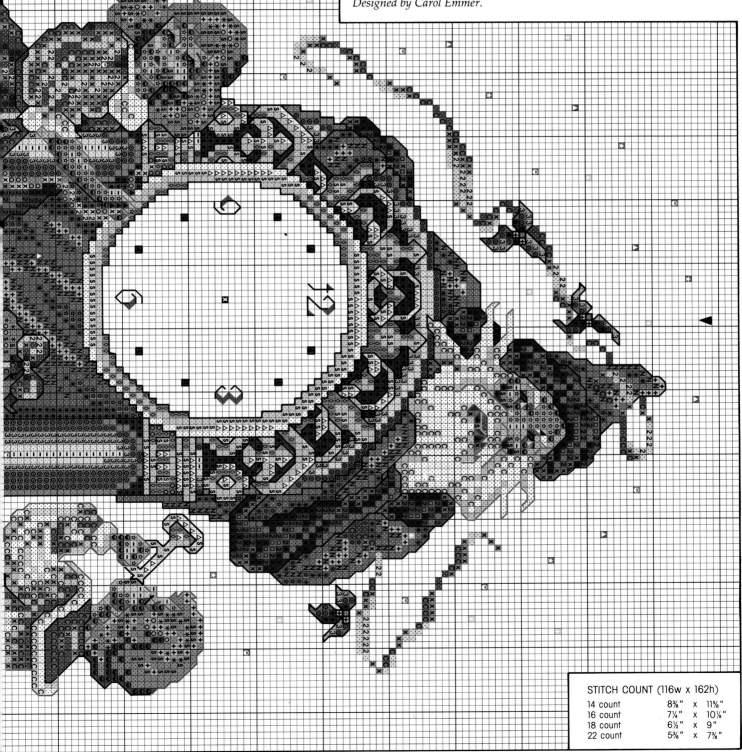

STITCH COUNT (116w x 162h)			
14 count	8⅜"	x	11⅝"
16 count	7¼"	x	10⅛"
18 count	6½"	x	9"
22 count	5⅜"	x	7⅜"

V is for Voices

#1 (48w x 66h)

#2 (44w x 41h)

#3 (90w x 55h)

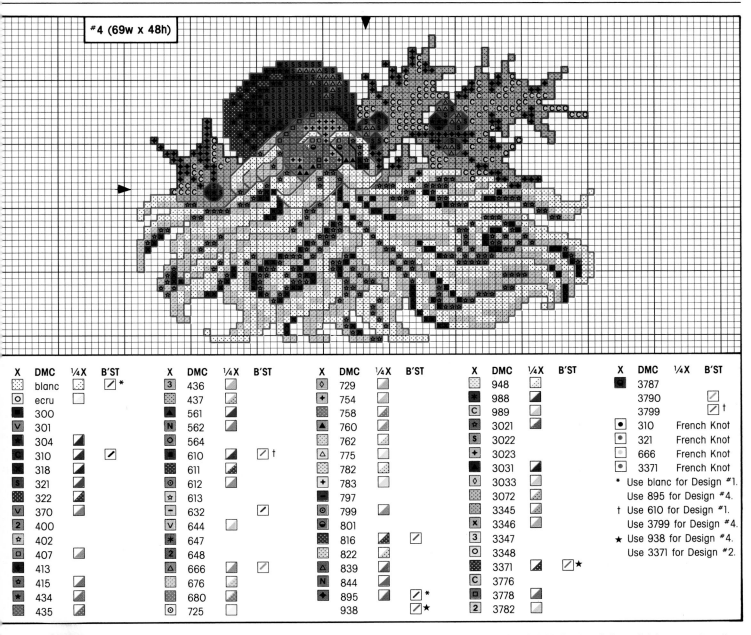

#4 (69w x 48h)

X	DMC	1/4X	B'ST	X	DMC	1/4X	B'ST	X	DMC	1/4X	B'ST	X	DMC	1/4X	B'ST	X	DMC	1/4X	B'ST
	blanc	✓	✓ *		436	✓			729	✓			948	✓			3787		
	ecru	✓			437	✓			754	✓			988	✓			3790		✓
	300				561	✓			758	✓			989	✓			3799		✓ †
	301				562	✓			760	✓			3021	✓			310	French Knot	
	304	✓			564				762	✓			3022				321	French Knot	
	310	✓	✓		610	✓	✓ †		775	✓			3023				666	French Knot	
	318	✓			611	✓			782	✓			3031				3371	French Knot	
	321	✓			612	✓			783	✓			3033						
	322	✓			613				797				3072						
	370	✓			632		✓		799	✓			3345	✓					
	400				644	✓			801				3346	✓					
	402				647				816	✓	✓		3347	✓					
	407	✓			648				822	✓			3348	✓					
	413				666	✓	✓		839	✓			3371	✓	✓ ★				
	415	✓			676	✓			844	✓			3776						
	434	✓			680	✓			895	✓	✓ *		3778	✓					
	435	✓			725				938		✓ ★		3782						

* Use blanc for Design #1.
  Use 895 for Design #4.
† Use 610 for Design #1.
  Use 3799 for Design #4.
★ Use 938 for Design #4.
  Use 3371 for Design #2.

Carolers' Sweatshirts (shown on pages 42-43): Each design was stitched over a 15" x 13" piece of 10 mesh waste canvas on a purchased sweatshirt with top of designs approximately 2" below bottom of neckband. Five strands of floss were used for Cross Stitch and 2 strands for Backstitch and French Knots.

Needlework adaptation by Donna Vermillion Giampa and Jane Chandler.

Working on Waste Canvas: Waste canvas is a special canvas that provides an evenweave grid for placing stitches on fabric. After the design is worked over the canvas, the canvas threads are removed leaving the design on the fabric. The canvas is available in several mesh sizes.

Cover edges of canvas with masking tape. Cut a piece of lightweight, non-fusible interfacing the same size as canvas to provide a firm stitching base.

Find desired stitching area on sweatshirt and mark center of area with a pin. Match center of canvas to pin. Use the blue threads in canvas to place canvas straight on shirt; pin canvas to shirt. Pin interfacing to wrong side of shirt. Baste all three thicknesses together as shown in **Fig. 1**.

Place shirt in a screw type hoop. We recommend a hoop that is large enough to encircle entire design. Using a sharp needle, work design, stitching from large holes to large holes.

Trim canvas to within ¾" of design. Dampen canvas until it becomes limp. Pull out canvas threads one at a time using tweezers (**Fig. 2**). Trim interfacing close to design.

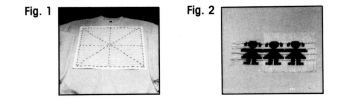

Fig. 1   **Fig. 2**

W for Wreaths

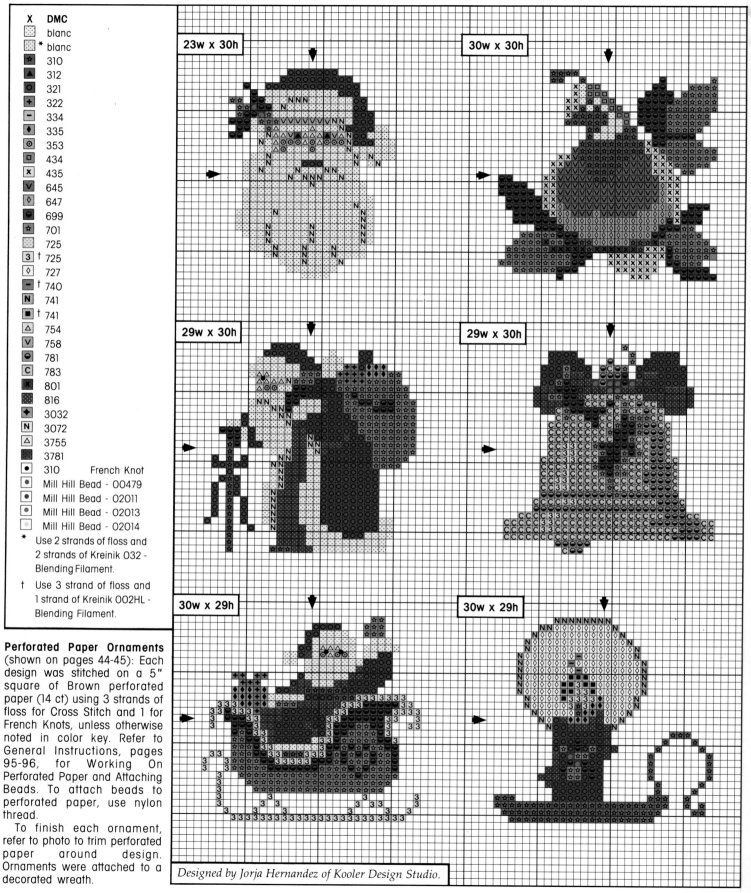

X	DMC	
	blanc	
	* blanc	
	310	
	312	
	321	
	322	
	334	
	335	
	353	
	434	
	435	
	645	
	647	
	699	
	701	
	725	
3	† 725	
	727	
	† 740	
N	741	
	† 741	
	754	
	758	
	781	
C	783	
	801	
	816	
	3032	
N	3072	
	3755	
	3781	
•	310	French Knot
	Mill Hill Bead - 00479	
	Mill Hill Bead - 02011	
	Mill Hill Bead - 02013	
	Mill Hill Bead - 02014	

* Use 2 strands of floss and
   2 strands of Kreinik 032 -
   Blending Filament.

† Use 3 strand of floss and
   1 strand of Kreinik 002HL -
   Blending Filament.

Perforated Paper Ornaments
(shown on pages 44-45): Each
design was stitched on a 5"
square of Brown perforated
paper (14 ct) using 3 strands of
floss for Cross Stitch and 1 for
French Knots, unless otherwise
noted in color key. Refer to
General Instructions, pages
95-96, for Working On
Perforated Paper and Attaching
Beads. To attach beads to
perforated paper, use nylon
thread.

To finish each ornament,
refer to photo to trim perforated
paper around design.
Ornaments were attached to a
decorated wreath.

Designed by Jorja Hernandez of Kooler Design Studio.

30w x 26h

29w x 29h

30w x 30h

29w x 30h

30w x 29h

30w x 30h

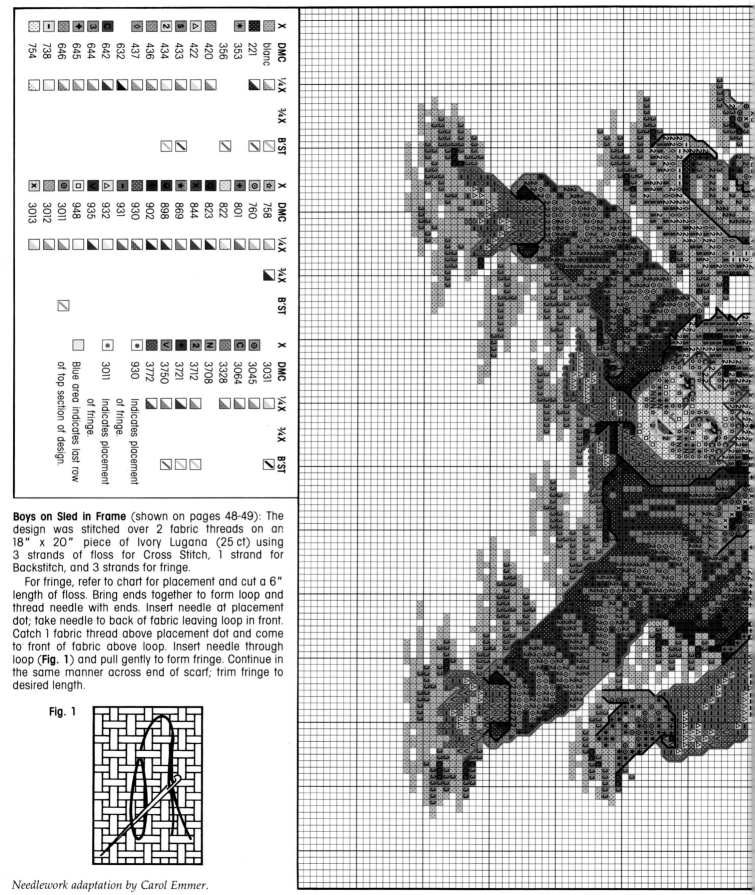

Boys on Sled in Frame (shown on pages 48-49): The design was stitched over 2 fabric threads on an 18" x 20" piece of Ivory Lugana (25 ct) using 3 strands of floss for Cross Stitch, 1 strand for Backstitch, and 3 strands for fringe.

For fringe, refer to chart for placement and cut a 6" length of floss. Bring ends together to form loop and thread needle with ends. Insert needle at placement dot; take needle to back of fabric leaving loop in front. Catch 1 fabric thread above placement dot and come to front of fabric above loop. Insert needle through loop (**Fig. 1**) and pull gently to form fringe. Continue in the same manner across end of scarf; trim fringe to desired length.

Fig. 1

Needlework adaptation by Carol Emmer.

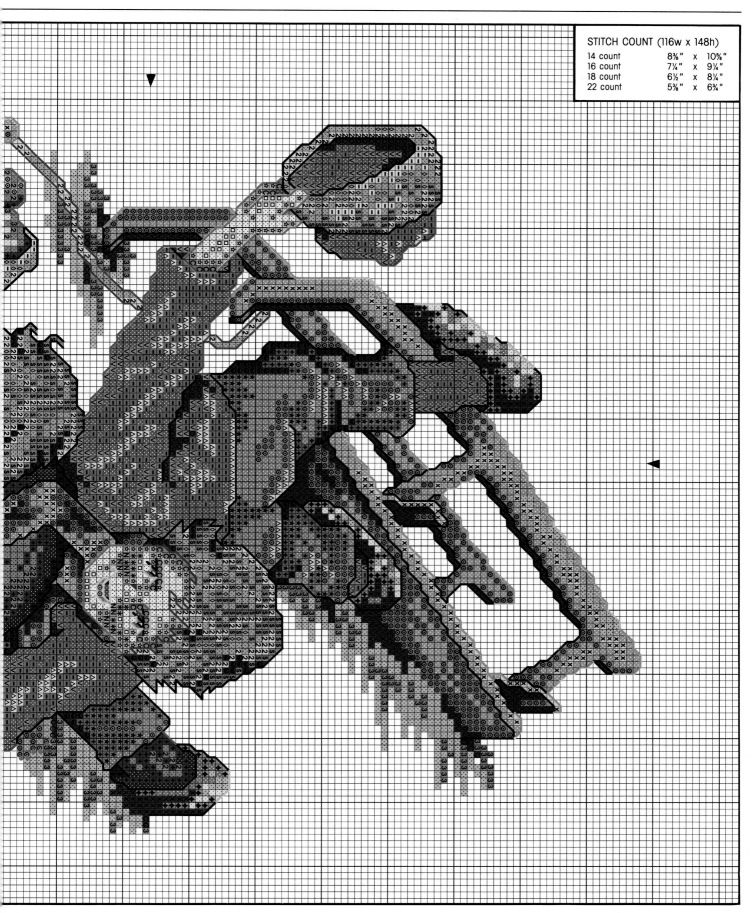

X is for Xmas

STITCH COUNT (79w x 264h)

14 count	5¾"	x	18⅞"
16 count	5"	x	16½"
18 count	4½"	x	14¾"
22 count	3⅝"	x	12"

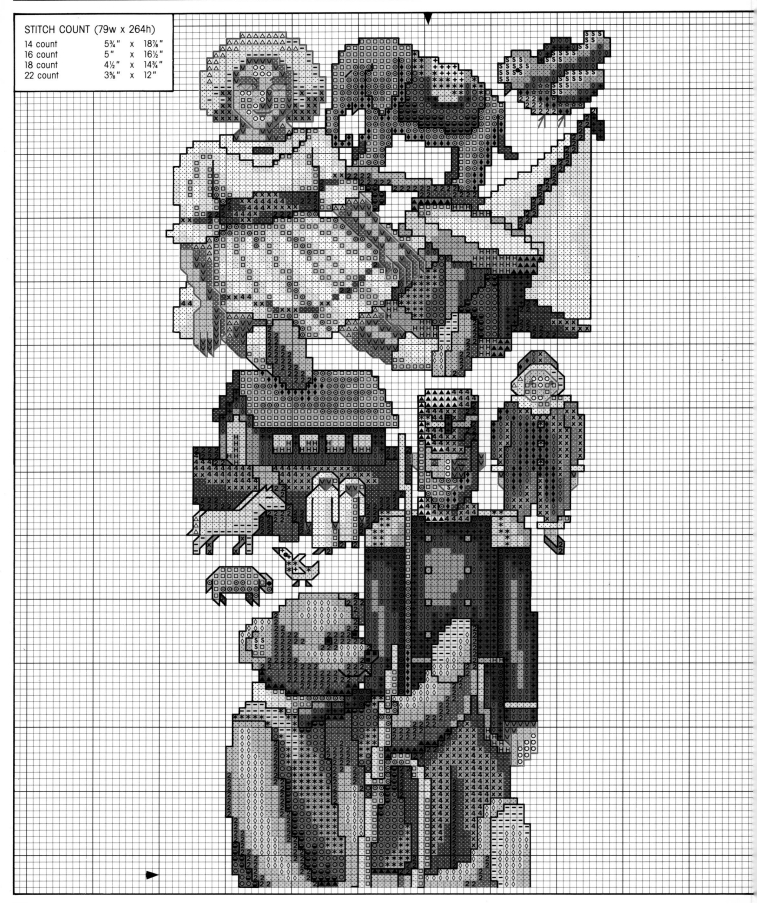

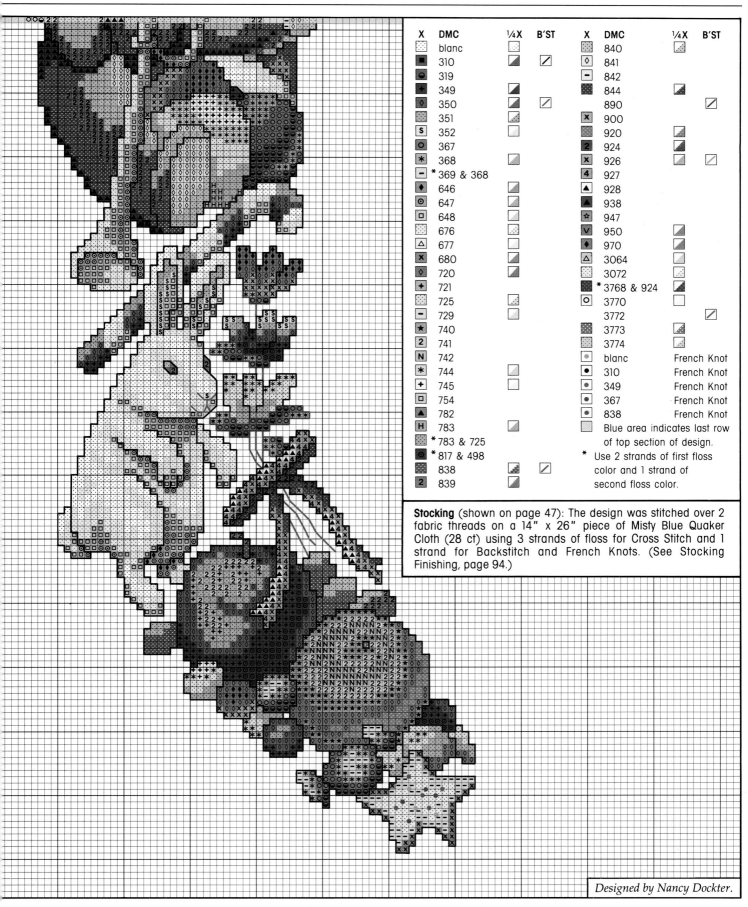

X	DMC	¼X	B'ST	X	DMC	¼X	B'ST
	blanc				840		
	310				841		
	319				842		
	349				844		
	350				890		
	351			X	900		
S	352			2	924		
	367			X	926		
	368			4	927		
-	*369 & 368				928		
	646				938		
	647				947		
	648			V	950		
	676				970		
	677				3064		
X	680				3072		
	720				*3768 & 924		
	721			O	3770		
	725				3772		
-	729				3773		
	740				3774		
2	741				blanc	French Knot	
N	742				310	French Knot	
	744				349	French Knot	
	745				367	French Knot	
	754				838	French Knot	
	782						
H	783						
	*783 & 725						
	*817 & 498						
	838						
2	839						

Blue area indicates last row of top section of design.

* Use 2 strands of first floss color and 1 strand of second floss color.

Stocking (shown on page 47): The design was stitched over 2 fabric threads on a 14" x 26" piece of Misty Blue Quaker Cloth (28 ct) using 3 strands of floss for Cross Stitch and 1 strand for Backstitch and French Knots. (See Stocking Finishing, page 94.)

Designed by Nancy Dockter.

X is for Xmas

Stocking chart on pages 92-93.

STOCKING FINISHING

For stocking, you will need tracing paper, 14" x 26" piece of Quaker Cloth for backing, two 14" x 26" pieces of coordinating fabric for lining, thread to match fabric, fabric marking pencil, and a 2" x 5" piece of Quaker Cloth for hanger.

Matching arrows to form one pattern, trace entire stocking pattern onto tracing paper; cut out pattern. Center pattern on wrong side of stitched piece; draw around pattern. Matching right sides and raw edges, pin stitched piece and backing fabric together.

Leaving top edge open, sew stitched piece and backing fabric together directly on drawn line; remove pins. Trim top edge along drawn line. Trim seam allowance to ½" and clip curves; turn stocking right side out. Press top edge of stocking ½" to wrong side.

For lining, match right sides and raw edges of lining fabric; pin place. Center pattern on wrong side of fabric; draw around pattern. Leaving top edge open, sew slightly inside drawn line; remove pins. Trim top edge along drawn line; trim seam allowance close to stitching. **Do not turn lining inside out.** Press top edge of lining ½" to wrong side.

For hanger, press each long edge of fabric strip ½" to center. Matching long edges, fold strip in half and sew close to folded edges. Matching short edges, fold hanger in half and whipstitch to inside of stocking at left seam.

With wrong sides facing, place lining inside stocking; whipstitch lining to stocking.

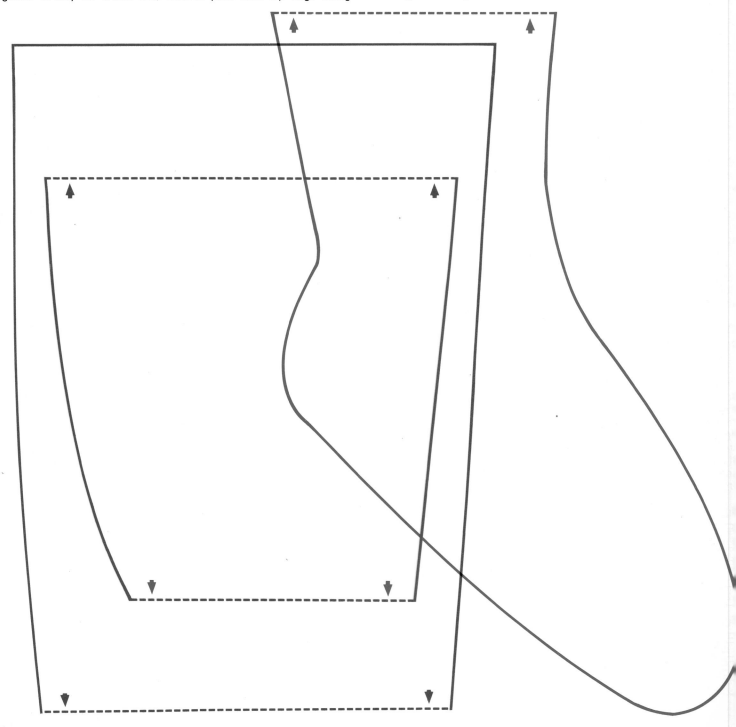

GENERAL INSTRUCTIONS

WORKING WITH CHARTS

How to Read Charts: Each of the designs is shown in chart form. Each colored square on the chart represents one Cross Stitch or one Half Cross Stitch. Each colored triangle on the chart represents one One-Quarter Stitch or one Three-Quarter Stitch. Black or colored dots represent French Knots. Colored ovals represent Lazy Daisy Stitches. The black or colored straight lines on the chart indicate Backstitch. When a French Knot, Lazy Daisy Stitch, or Backstitch covers a square, the symbol is omitted.

Each chart is accompanied by a color key. This key indicates the color of floss to use for each stitch on the chart. The headings on the color key are for Cross Stitch (**X**), DMC color number (**DMC**), Quarter Stitch (**¼X**), Three-Quarter Stitch (**¾X**), Half Cross Stitch (**½X**), and Backstitch (**B'ST**). Color key columns should be read vertically and horizontally to determine type of stitch and floss color.

Where to Start: The horizontal and vertical centers of each charted design are shown by arrows. You may start at any point on the charted design, but be sure the design will be centered on the fabric. Locate the center of fabric by folding in half, top to bottom and again left to right. On the charted design, count the number of squares (stitches) from the center of the chart to where you wish to start. Then from the fabric's center, find your starting point by counting out the same number of fabric threads (stitches).

STITCH DIAGRAMS

Counted Cross Stitch (X): Work one Cross Stitch to correspond to each colored square on the chart. For horizontal rows, work stitches in two journeys (**Fig. 1**). For vertical rows, complete each stitch as shown (**Fig. 2**). When working over two fabric threads, work Cross Stitch as shown in **Fig. 3**. When the chart shows a Backstitch crossing a colored square (**Fig. 4**), a Cross Stitch should be worked first; then the Backstitch (**Fig. 9 or 10**) should be worked on top of the Cross Stitch.

Fig. 1

Fig. 2

Fig. 3

Fig. 4

Quarter Stitch (¼X and ¾X): Quarter Stitches are denoted by triangular shapes of color on the chart and on the color key. Come up at 1 (**Fig. 5**); then split fabric thread to go down at 2. When stitches 1-4 are worked in the same color, the resulting stitch is called a Three-Quarter Stitch (**¾X**). **Fig. 6** shows the technique for Quarter Stitch when working over two fabric threads.

Fig. 5

Fig. 6

Half Cross Stitch (½X): This stitch is one journey of the Cross Stitch and is worked from lower left to upper right as shown in **Fig. 7**. When working over two fabric threads, work Half Cross Stitch as shown in **Fig. 8**.

Fig. 7

Fig. 8

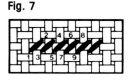

Backstitch (B'ST): For outline detail, Backstitch (shown on chart and on color key by black or colored straight lines) should be worked after the design has been completed (**Fig. 9**). When working over two fabric threads, work Backstitch as shown in **Fig. 10**.

Fig. 9

Fig. 10

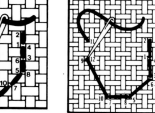

French Knot: Bring needle up at 1. Wrap floss once around needle and insert needle at 2, holding end of floss with non-stitching fingers (**Fig. 11**). Tighten knot; then pull needle through fabric, holding floss until it must be released. For larger knot, use more strands; wrap only once.

Fig. 11

Lazy Daisy Stitch: Bring needle up at 1 and make a loop. Go down at 1 and come up at 2, keeping floss below point of needle (**Fig. 12**). Pull needle through and go down at 2 to anchor loop, completing stitch. (**Note:** To support stitches, it may be helpful to go down in edge of next fabric thread when anchoring loop.)

Fig. 12

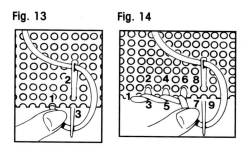

Blanket Stitch: Bring needle up at 1, go down at 2 and come up at 3, keeping the floss below the point of the needle (**Fig. 13**). Continue working in this manner, going down at even numbers and coming up at odd numbers (**Fig. 14**).

Fig. 13 **Fig. 14**

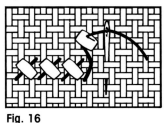

Attaching Beads: Refer to chart for bead placement and sew bead in place using a fine needle that will pass through bead. Bring needle up at 1, go down at 2 making a Half Cross Stitch (**Fig. 15**). Secure floss on back or move to next bead. When working on perforated paper, sew bead in place as shown in **Fig. 16**.

Fig. 15

Fig. 16

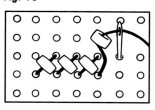

Continued on page 96

STITCHING TIPS

Working Over Two Fabric Threads: Use the sewing method instead of the stab method when working over two fabric threads. To use the sewing method, keep your stitching hand on the right side of the fabric (instead of stabbing the fabric with the needle and taking your stitching hand to the back of the fabric to pick up the needle). With the sewing method, you take the needle down and up with one stroke instead of two. To add support to stitches, it is important that the first Cross Stitch is placed on the fabric with stitch 1-2 beginning and ending where a vertical fabric thread crosses over a horizontal fabric thread (**Fig. 17**). When the first stitch is in the correct position, the entire design will be placed properly, with vertical fabric threads supporting each stitch.

Fig. 17

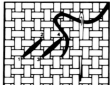

Working on Perforated Paper: Perforated paper has a right side and a wrong side. The right side is smoother and stitching should be done on this side. To find the center, do not fold paper; use a ruler and mark lightly with a pencil or count holes. Perforated paper will tear if handled roughly; therefore, hold the paper flat while stitching and do not use a hoop. Begin and end stitching by running floss under several stitches on back; never tie knots. Use the stab method when stitching and keep stitching tension consistent. Thread pulled too tightly may tear the paper. Carry floss across back as little as possible.

JAR LID FINISHING

For jar lid, use **outer edge** of jar lid for pattern and draw a circle on adhesive mounting board. Cutting slightly inside drawn line, cut out circle. Using **opening** of jar lid for pattern, cut a circle of batting. Remove paper from adhesive board; center batting on adhesive board and press in place. Center stitched piece on batting and press edges onto adhesive board; cut edges close to board. Glue board inside jar lid. Refer to photo to trim jar lid edge as desired.

Instructions tested and photo items made by Janet Akins, Debbie Bashaw, Marsha Besancon, Vicky Bishop, Cecilia Carswell, Nancy Coriden, Marilyn Fendley, Chrys Harvey, Muriel Hicks, Pat Johnson, Velda Leuders, Terri Lowe, Wes Nuckolls, Martha Nolan, Sara Olds, Dave Ann Pennington, Mary Phinney, Sandy Pigue, Liz Pounders, Susan Sego, Karen Sisco, Opal Steen, Karen Tyler, Trish Vines, Jane Walker, and Marie Williford.